MW00989729

JOHN RITCHIE

TABERNACLE
IN THE
WILDERNESS

*A Study of Christ in the Tabernacle,
the Offerings, and the Priesthood*

Grand Rapids, MI 49501

Tabernacle in the Wilderness: A Study of Christ in the Tabernacle, the Offerings, and the Priesthood

Published in 1982 by Kregel Publications, a division of Kregel, Inc., P.O. Box 2607, Grand Rapids, MI 49501.

Cover design: Frank Gutbrod

Library of Congress Cataloging-in-Publication Data
Ritchie, John.
    Tabernacle in the wilderness: A study of Christ in the tabernacle, the offerings, and the priesthood / by John Ritchie.
        p.   cm.
    Originally published: New ed., rev. and enl. Kilmarnock, Scotland. J. Ritchie, 1891.
    1. Tabernacle—Typology.   2. Typology (Theology).
I. Title.
BM654.R6   1982   221'.6'4   82-178
                                                  AACR2
ISBN 0-8254-3616-8

Printed in the United States of America

8 9 0 11 12 / 07 06 05 04 03

CONTENTS

FOREWORD

If you like a book with practical simply-stated truths, yet deeply enriching, John Ritchie's *The Tabernacle in the Wilderness* is for you! What a thrilling parallel between the Old Testament Tabernacle and a Christian's daily life is given here! If you have ever wondered why each detail of the Tabernacle had to be carried out so particularly, Mr. Ritchie will tell you.

The explanation of each vital element of the Tabernacle and how it applies to the reader's every day life is fascinating. You will be amazed how every facet of the Tabernacle is relevant to your life. As you read you will catch yourself being drawn to the desert. Maybe bringing a lamb, maybe putting up the poles, or maybe waiting expectantly in the outer court. Mr. Ritchie causes you to desire to bow your knee to the majesty, power, and love of God.

The author has great ability to write simply. He also writes so interestingly that you will not want to stop at the chapter's end. As you come to the Holy of Holies, your life cannot be the same for Mr. Ritchie causes you to catch a glimpse of the Holiness of God. You will view Christ on the cross, and then risen and glorified. Through the pen of this Holy Spirit-directed author you should be drawn to a new awareness of the orderliness and holiness God desires in our lives.

Whether the reader be a pastor, teacher, or earnest Christian, he should come from its pages refreshed and rejoicing.

Arnold J. Fair

INTRODUCTION

I desire to state, in a few words, the object we have in view in coming together to search and meditate on the typical teaching of the Tabernacle. It is not to instruct those who have been searching and inquiring into this subject for years, and who can therefore rejoice in its riches ; nor is it to expound minutely or go into all the details of this deeply-important portion of the Word of God. Those who do so will find it an interesting study, and a large and fruitful field for deep searching and meditation. Our desire is rather to guide the dear lambs of the Lord's flock—those who have been recently converted to God—to these green pastures, and, as the Holy Spirit may show them, to seek to point out a few of the precious things concerning the person and work of Christ, as they are found lying on the surface of these types, trusting that all may be sufficiently interested to dig deeper into the mine for themselves.

I suppose we have all been struck, on reading our Bibles, to find how much of that Book is occupied with types. The first five books are almost entirely typical, and many other parts of the Word abound in them. This was the Lord's method of teaching His people in days of old. And when the Lord Jesus was here on earth, we all remember how often He used those types to illustrate the truths He taught. (See John 3:14 ; 6:31-33.)

We cannot for one moment entertain the infidel and foolish speculations of some would-be wise men about those parts of the Word of God. They would like to make us believe that they were only intended for patriarchs and

Israelites, and that we can derive little or no profit from
them ; indeed, some are now saying that they form no
part of the inspired Scriptures at all ! But the youngest of
us knows better. We prize them as part of our Father's
holy Word, of which it is written—" All Scripture is
given by inspiration of God (or is God-breathed), and is
profitable," (2 Tim. 3:16) ; and " Whatsoever things
were written aforetime were written for our learning,"
(Rom. 15:4)   The first of these Scriptures assures us
that the typical books are *from* God ; the latter, that
they are *for* us. In our unconverted days, we saw no
beauty in long chapters about bullocks and altars ; and
we either passed them by unread, or we were glad when
we got through them. Like a young lady of whom I have
read, who was presented with a book and asked to read
it carefully. Out of courtesy to the giver, she did so, but
found it uninteresting and very dry. By and by, she
became acquainted with the author, loved him, and became
his bride. With what interest and pleasure she read the
same book then ! How eagerly each line was scanned,
each page perused ! To her it was a new book. And why ?
Because she knew and loved the one who wrote it. So it
is now with God's saints. They know God ; they love
His Book. The types are God's own pictures, and they
point forward to Christ.

I remember seeing in this city several years ago a
well-marked Bible. It belonged to a precious saint, who
has since gone home to be with her Lord. Along the
margin of one of the typical books the following two
lines were written :

IN THE OLD TESTAMENT THE NEW LIES HID ;

IN THE NEW TESTAMENT THE OLD LIES OPEN.

I thought this was very sweet. It expresses most
simply the meaning of the types and how we may understand them. It is the Jesus of the New Testament that

we see in the types of the Old ; Jesus in the lamb, the altar, the priest ; Jesus in the varied glories of His Person and the varied aspects of His work. The believer who has most acquaintance with the Lord Jesus, who loves Him best, will see most beauty in the types. Love is quick-sighted : it sees beauties and perfections in its object, where a stranger's eye sees none. We look closely at those we love ; the lineaments of the countenance, the ways, the habits, and the resorts of the loved one, are all observed. The deeper our appreciation is of Jesus, the closer we will study each type that speaks to us of Him. Remember, they are no mere rough sketches ; each detail will bear the closest inspection, and the deeper we search the more we shall find that the types are the work of God, and, like Him of Whom they speak, unsearchable in their riches.

I have sometimes thought how real they must have been to the Lord Jesus as He read them. What feelings must have filled His holy soul, as He mused on such types as the killing of the paschal lamb and the burning of the sin-offering without the camp, knowing as He did, that they had to be fulfilled in Himself.

The types of GENESIS are chiefly *dispensational.* Turn to chapter I. Here in ver. 1 we have the story of the Creation. Then the six days' work, in the forming of earth, for man's habitation, beginning with the giving of light, and ending with the creation of man in the image of God. The story is most interesting ; but how very much more so when we learn that it is a figure of the new creation (see 2 Cor. 5:17 ; Eph. 2:10). It illustrates the work of God, by His Word and Spirit, in a sinner's soul, from the day that the entrance of God's Word gives light, on to the perfect day when he shall be presented in the image of the heavenly. Genesis 2 introduces Adam and Eve. Adam " is the figure of Him that was to come " (Rom. 5:14), " the last Adam " (1 Cor. 15:45), the Head of the new creation ; and Eve, a type of the Church, His Bride (Gen. 2:21-23, with Eph. 5:30-32).

The story of Hagar, the home-bringing of Isaac's bride, and Joseph's rejection by his brethren, all abound in typical truth.

EXODUS is the Book of REDEMPTION. The Passover, the Red Sea, and the Tabernacle with its furniture, are all types of redemption and its results to the people of God.

LEVITICUS is the Book of the PRIESTS. It chiefly consists of types showing the way of worship and access to God, and how communion with God may be maintained, or restored when broken, and so on.

May the Risen One, who drew near to the two weary travellers on the Emmaus road, and, " beginning at *Moses*, expounded to them in all the Scriptures the things concerning Himself," draw near to us and reveal Himself, while we meditate on these very portions of His Word. So shall our heart burn within us, and we shall go on with quickened step toward our home.

TABERNACLE
IN THE
WILDERNESS

The Nation's History

A word on the history of this favored people in whose midst the Tabernacle was. Turn to Exodus 1. Here we have a picture of Israel in bondage. They had no Tabernacle, no glory-cloud there. Like the unconverted sinner, they were slaves ; they lived without God. Yet He loved them, and, faithful to His promise, He redeemed them. Exodus 12 shows their redemption. It was their birthday as a redeemed people.

Next comes their separation to God. The Red Sea opened to *let* them out of Egypt's power, and closed behind them to *keep* them out of it for ever. They were brought out to be alone with God in the desert. Here it was, far away from Egypt's altars and its gods, that God came down to dwell among them. Here it was that the Tabernacle was pitched. Let us learn a lesson from this. No believer who tarries in Egypt, need expect to apprehend the typical teaching of the Tabernacle. So long as a child of God is governed by the world's maxims and mixed up with its abominations, he can know but little of communion with his God. The promise, " I will dwell in them," is closely followed by the precept, " Come out from among them, and be ye separate " (2 Cor. 6:16-17). It is vain to sigh and cry over one's barrenness and lack of communion, and still remain in friendship with the world. If God's child can afford to forfeit the sunshine of his Father's face to gain the pleasures of the world ; if he

can coldly barter the friendship of his God for that of the
enemies of the Cross, he has no just reason to complain
of his bargain. If he know not the fellowship of the Lord's
redeemed encamped around His Tabernacle, let him heed
the call, " Come out from among them, and be ye separate,
. . . and *I* will receive you, saith the Lord."

Tabernacle, Literally and Typically

The Tabernacle was the dwelling-place of JEHOVAH
—God of Israel. It stood in the center of the twelve
tribes, facing the east. The cloud abode above, and the
glory continuously dwelt within its inner circle. To the
nations around, it must have appeared a very common-
looking edifice, more resembling a huge coffin, than the
temple of Israel's God, the palace of their King.

It consisted of three distinct circles. First, the Outer
Court, 100 cubits long by 50 wide.   It was surrounded
by an hanging of fine linen, and within it stood the altar
of Burnt-offering and the Laver. The Tabernacle proper
stood in the western end of this enclosure. It was divided
into two apartments. The first was called the Holy Place.
This was 20 cubits long by 10 wide.   It contained the
altar of incense, the table of shew-bread, and the golden
candlestick. . A curtain hung on four pillars, called the
veil, divided between the Holy Place and the Holiest of all.
The Holiest was a square apartment, 10 cubits long by 10
wide.   Within it, stood the Ark of the Covenant, with
the Mercy Seat and Cherubim, the cloud of glory resting
between them.

The twelve tribes were gathered around, each in its
divinely-ordered place. The camp consisted of probably
over two million souls.

When Moses was in the mount with God, he was

shown a pattern of the Tabernacle, and he also received instructions how each part of it was to be made. Not one single pin or knop was omitted in the Divine instructions, and Moses was repeatedly told to adhere strictly to them in all their details (Exod. 25:40 ; 26:30). The house was God's, and He ordered it. Moses, as a faithful servant, obeyed. It would be well for us to-day if all the servants of Christ would remember that the Lord has not been less careful about the building of His Church. He has given the Divine pattern and the most minute instructions as to how His House on earth is to be ordered (see 1 Cor. ; 1 Tim.). this remains the unrepealed, unchanging will of God for His People's obedience throughout the whole of the Church's earthly history until the Lord comes.

The Tabernacle was God's first dwelling-place on earth. He *walked* in the company of Adam in Eden. He *visited* Abraham at Mamre, but had no dwelling-place there. Here He comes down to *dwell* with His redeemed, and from then till now, He has had a dwelling-place on earth. After the Tabernacle, the Temple in the land (2 Chron. 6:3-6) ;   and when its day was past, the Son from the Father's bosom came. God was manifest in the flesh, "the Word became flesh, and *tabernacled* among us" (John 1:14 R.V.). The glory of God was manifest in the temple of His Body. Next came the Church—a spiritual house, an holy temple, built of living stones. This is the present dwelling-place of God on earth. No house, however gorgeous, no temple made with hands however grand, can claim the honour of being "the House of God." He dwelleth not in temples made with hands. But "where two or three" of His ransomed saints are found gathered together in the Name of the Lord Jesus Christ, *there* He is in their midst (Matt. 18: 20). This is His rest ; here will He dwell, for He has

desired it   (Psa. 132:14).   And by and by, when time
and sin and death shall be no more, when wilderness
toils and tears are past, the last foe vanquished, and God
shall be all in all, then shall "the Tabernacle of God be
with men, and He will dwell with them, and they shall be
His people " (Rev. 21:3).

TYPICALLY, the Tabernacle pointed onward to Christ.
In His Temple every part of it uttered His glory (Psa.
29:9).   Christ is all. The glories of His Person and
work are stamped on every part of it, from the Ark of the
Covenant within the veil, to the smallest pin and cord of
its outer Court. This will be seen more clearly, as we look
at its several parts.

It is also a figure of the wilderness condition of the
Church of God—*in* the world, but not *of* the world.

Freewill Offerings

The whole of the materials of which the Tabernacle
was built were the free-will offerings of the people of
God. No stranger or alien's gold was allowed to adorn
the dwelling-place of Israel's God. An unconverted
sinner's gifts are not accepted by the Lord, nor ought they
to be mingled with the offerings of the saints. Christendom
has deeply sinned in this. The world supports the nominal
Church, and wealthy worldlings are its pillars. Ill-gotten
gain, extorted from carnal men and sanctified in the Name
of God, is used to build religious temples in which the
pride and vanity of man may be displayed. With such
sacrifices God is *not* well pleased ; they savour of the
offering of Cain, and from God they have no respect. God
is a bountiful *Giver* ; and those who have been the reci-
pients of the riches of His grace, may well reflect His
character. The sense of God's goodness was present to
His people's hearts ; redemption and its results they had

tasted the sweetness of. They were in the dew of their
youth, and they gave, and gave their very best to God.
Rulers brought their precious stones and spices ; women
brought their bracelets and their jewels ; and those who
had no wealth to give, showed their love in labor. Strong
men felled the shittim trees, and wise-hearted women
spun. Morning after morning (Exodus 36:3), the gifts
of willing hearts poured in, in such abundance, too, that
Moses had to bid them cease. " For the stuff they had was
sufficient for all the work to make it, and *too much* "
(Exodus 36:7). Lovely grace ! It reminds us of the early
days of the Church of God, when mammon had lost its
hold, and the wealth of saints was given to God (*see* Acts 2).
How sad the change in the days of Malachi the prophet !
The people had departed from the Lord. They had lost
the sense of His goodness ; and they asked, " Wherein
hast Thou loved us ? " (Mal. 1:2). They brought the
lame and diseased of their bullocks to God's altar, and
kept the good ones for themselves. None would open a
door or kindle a fire for God, without being paid for his
work. And when to this very people the Son of God
appeared, they valued and sold Him for thirty pieces of
silver.

The Workmen

(Exodus 31:1-6)

Bezaleel and Aholiab were called and fitted for the
work, the former from the tribe of Judah—the royal
tribe (Heb. 7:14) ; the *first* also on the march (Num. 10:
14) ; the latter from the tribe of Dan, the *last* in the
camp. Thus does the Lord show us that He can find His
" chosen vessels " wheresoever He listeth. He called one
Apostle from the feet of Gamaliel and another from his
fishing boat on Galilee's Lake, and linked them together

as the Apostle of the circumcision and of the Gentiles
(Gal. 2:8).   And those whom He thus Calls, He fits for
His service. This is more than man can do. " Every one
whose heart stirred him up, came to the work to do it "
(Exodus 36:2).   Willing hearts caused willing hands to
work for God. So will they yet. A willing heart—a mind
to work—is the crying need of the present hour. Cold-
hearted saints will always find some lame excuse for
idleness ; but hearts a-glow with the love of Jesus will
easily find work to do for Him. God is building His
heavenly tent. Now is the opportunity for His saints to
show their love. Nothing really given *to* God or done *for*
Him with single eye, will be forgotten on a coming day.

> " Deeds of merit as we thought them,
>   *He* will tell us were but sin ;
> Little acts we had forgotten,
>   He will own were done for Him."

The Court

(Exodus 27:9-15)

The order in which the commands concerning the
Tabernacle and its vessels were given by Jehovah to
Moses, as also the order in which they were made and
placed, was from *within to without* (see Exodus 25 and
40), beginning with the Ark of the Covenant within the
Holiest, and ending with the Court and its gates without.

A descending line of typical truth is thus brought
before us. The order is *from* God *to* man. It reminds us
of the path of the Son of God—down from the bosom of
the Father to the manger of Bethlehem and the Cross of
Calvary, where He reached the sinner in all his guilt and
need.

The order in which our souls apprehend the truth is
from *without to within.* We begin with the Court and its

gate, and travel inward past the brazen altar and the laver, and onward till we reach the throne of God.

This will at once be apparent to us when we remember that, as sinners, our place is " without God " and " afar off " (Eph. 2:12-13). Our first apprehensions of Jesus are therefore suited to that condition.

It does not concern the guilty sinner how he may worship or commune with God. It is not the golden altar or the table that his soul seeks after then. Convicted and consciously lost, the cry of the awakened sinner is, " How can I be saved ? " and the Divine and all-sufficient answer from the lips of Jesus is, " I am *the* Door : by Me if any man enter in, he *shall be saved* " (John 10:9).

Once inside the gate, we go on to learn of Jesus as the Altar, the Sacrifice, and the Priest. We pass within the Holy Place to worship God and to " behold the beauty of the Lord " within His dwelling-place. I speak now of our apprehension of the truth, not of our standing in Christ. The youngest babe in the family of God has Christ, and having Christ, has all. The aged saint can have no more than Christ ; the babe has nothing less. The difference lies in the experimental knowledge of Him. The babe has only known Him, it may be, a few days ; the aged pilgrim has leaned on His arm for years, and knows His restoring and upholding, as well as His saving power.

We shall now pursue our subject thus, and begin by looking at the Court of the Tabernacle.

The Court was an open space, 100 cubits long by 50 cubits wide surrounded by a hanging of fine twined linen, supported by 56 pillars. Each pillar stood in a socket of brass (or copper), and was crowned with silver ; hooks of silver upheld the curtains, and rods of silver connected the pillars. An unbroken line of silver and fine linen went thus round about the Court. On the eastern

side was the gate. It was 20 cubits wide and consisted of
an embroidered hanging of blue, purple, and scarlet, and
fine twined linen. It was suspended on four pillars.   This
was the only entrance to the dwelling-place of Israel's God,
and he who would enter there, must submit to do so in
God's appointed way. There was no choice, no variety.
The truth taught here is very solemn. May we have ears
to hear.

The Court may be looked at as illustrative of that
outermost circle of blessing which the sinner consciously
enters when by faith he sees Jesus as the Door of Salvation.
The holy places—figures of the heavens   (Heb. 9:24)—
and his position there as a worshipper, he may not yet
understand, but he knows himself *saved,* delivered from
the wrath to come, and within, the circle of the family of
God, where grace and mercy can deal with him. Even to
be there—the very lowest view of the place and portion of
a saint—is most blessed. No wonder that David sang,
" A day in Thy *courts* is better than a thousand. I would
rather be a doorkeeper (margin, ' sit on the threshold') in
the house of my God, than dwell in the tents of wickedness " (Psalm 84:10).

Sinner ! you do not know what you are losing by
staying outside the gate. There are joys and pleasures
within, such as you can never know in the "tents of
wickedness." A little while, and these tents shall be
overthrown ; the unsatisfying and delusive charms of a
godless world, shall all be gone for ever. Full well the
happy saint may sing, " Blessed is the man whom Thou
choosest, and causest to approach unto Thee, that he may
dwell in Thy *courts*: we shall be SATISFIED with the
goodness of Thy house " (Psalm 65:4).

We are not told of what material the pillars were made ;
we need not therefore pry into God's secrets, or seem to be
wise where He has been silent. The silence signifies that

they are something to be looked away from. The copper
represents God in righteousness judging sin. The silver
speaks of redemption through the blood of Christ. The
hangings of the Court were of fine twined linen. The
Bride of the Lamb is said to be " arrayed in fine linen,
clean and white (' bright and pure '), for the fine linen is
the righteousness (' righteous acts ') of saints " (Rev. 19
8, Revised Version.) Fine linen, then, is the emblem of
righteousness. But naturally, and apart from Christ, the
saints had no such righteousness. Their very best was
" filthy rags " (Isa. 64:6). Such is the emblem chosen
by the Spirit of God to show the best of human righteousness, in contrast with what is Divine. " FINE LINEN,
CLEAN AND WHITE "—" FILTHY RAGS." How striking the
contrast ! How vast the difference ! Let the sinner ponder
it, and ask himself, in which he stands before a holy God ?
There has been only One down here below, in whose life
and ways the linen bright and pure was seen in its unsullied
brightness. He was " Jesus Christ the Righteous." No
coarse threads, no taints of unrighteousness were in Him.
Jesus was perfect : perfect in His devotedness to God,
perfect in His righteousness toward man. To Him, and
Him alone, the fine linen belonged by right. In Him, and
Him alone, it was fully, perfectly and continually manifested here. Men around Him saw its brightness, and
they shunned it. It was a continual rebuke to the Scribes
and Pharisees—the religious leaders of that day—and they
hated it ; yet there He stood, the Righteous One amid the
unrighteous, the Holy amid the unclean, revealing and
displaying such righteousness and holiness as are of God.
The holy life of Jesus here on earth, apart from the shedding
of His Blood, could have brought no salvation, no comfort
to the sinner. How foolish then is the thought, how utterly
false is the doctrine, now, alas, so widely spread throughout Christendom, that the life of Jesus was given us as

an example, and that by copying it man may reach the
Kingdom of God! Ah no ; it is as we draw near and gaze
on Him—as we place our own "filthy rags" of human
righteousness alongside the hanging of linen, pure and
white, that we learn what we really are. So long as Job was
reasoning and arguing with his fellow-men, he could say :
" My righteousness I hold fast and will not let it go " ; but,
when face to face with God, he had to own—" Mine eye
seeth *Thee*, therefore I ABHOR MYSELF " (Job. 42:5, 6).

Sinner, have you ever seen yourself thus ? Have you
ever stood with closed mouth, convicted and condemned,
at the outside of that circle of righteousness surrounding
the dwelling-place of God ? If such be the righteousness
that God demands from those who enter the courts of
His Holiness, then you have not got it. You must be shut
out from God for ever, on the ground of righteousness.
The claims of God can never be lowered ; the curtain is
five cubits high, the same all round. There is no loophole,
no ill-adjusted corner through which you may slip un-
awares. If you are trusting to the mercy of God, and
forgetting His holiness and His righteousness, you are
making a fatal mistake. You are seeking to " climb up
some other way " to reach the Kingdom of God. If you
expect to go to Heaven by works, you are attempting
to break down the claims of God, and trample the curtain
of linen to the ground. The " *great white throne* " of
judgment, to be set up in eternity, will bear witness to
the same truth as that fine linen curtain. The dead who
stand before that throne, will be judged according to their
works. The open books bring back to view the record
of earthly lives of those who " had pleasure in unrighteousness." There will not be one in all that vast assembly
who can claim a place in Heaven on the ground of human
righteousness. They are all condemned, and cast into the
burning lake.

The Gate

(Exodus 27:16-17)

In front of the Tabernacle, in the center of the Court, facing the east, was *the gate*. The east in Scripture is connected with rising light. The camp of Judah was commanded to pitch on the east, "toward the rising of the sun" (Num. 2:3). The beams of the rising sun would thus fall first upon the gate, revealing its colours, and showing the way of approach to God. There was no back or side entrance : he who entered it must do so in the light.

Men naturally love the darkness, because of their evil deeds. The light makes manifest what man is. The sinner must be exposed before he can be saved : he must enter God's appointed gate in the full consciousness that he is a sinner ; there must be no shirking of the light, no covering or hiding of his state. And this is why so many of the self-righteous refuse the way of God. They will not submit to be searched and humbled in the light of God, or to take salvation such as God has provided ; therefore, they devise ways of their own. Cain was the first of these. He blinked the fact that he was a fallen man, and sought in the darkness, a way to God, apart from shed blood. Others followed in his steps ; and "the way of Cain" is trodden by thousands of self-righteous souls, who seek a way to God apart from the blood of the Lamb. The end of all such ways is death : the blackness of darkness for ever.

The gate was the *only* way of access to God. Why was there only one ? Because God had provided no more, and no one had any right to find fault with God's arrangement. Why was it on the east ? Because God has so appointed. It was all of His doing, all of His providing, and He, as Sovereign, had a right to do as He pleased. How needful it is to remember this. Men all around us are questioning God's ways and sitting in judgment upon them. They are questioning His existence, questioning His ability, questioning the truthfulness and the authority of His Word. To contend for the one gate is counted "bigotry." To stand up for the truth of God is branded as "narrow-mindedness." "If a man be sincere, no matter what he believes, he will surely go to Heaven" is the popular creed. Although men differ in their belief, yet, somehow, they will all arrive at the same happy end at last: sceptics and believers, sinners and saints, all the same, is the substance of this popular Gospel. False as it is, this most palatable fable is preached from many pulpits, and greedily devoured by the people. The man who conjures up the greatest falsehood, and shows the ways of access to Heaven to be most diverse, is considered the "charitable man"; and he who contends that God has only *one* way whereby a sinner can draw nigh, and that there is "none other name" than the Name of Jesus whereby the lost may be saved, is barely tolerated. Yet, such is the ever-abiding truth of God, and he who rejects or denies it, will find out his mistake by and by.

The gate was for *all*: the prince and the beggar alike. The grey-haired father and the little child might enter it side by side. So it is with Jesus Christ. The thief of Calvary, the woman of the city, and Saul the Pharisee, passed through the same gate, and were all saved with the "common salvation."

The gate was *wide*, but low. It was twenty cubits wide by five high. It may be contrasted with the door of the Holy Place, the dimensions of which were ten cubits high by ten cubits wide. The area of both is alike, but the door is twice the height and only half the width of the gate. the leading thought in the door is *height*, in the gate, *width*. The application is evident. The Holy Place was only for the priests. Others were not allowed to enter there. Its entrance was therefore a narrow one. The privileges of the family of God are not for the world ; the unconverted sinner is not admitted within the range of them. The door of the Church of God—His assembly on earth—ought to be no wider than to admit of those whom God has called to be there. The unconverted and the defiled are not allowed to enter. It is not so with the Gospel. The gate of the Court was *wide*, and any or all might enter there. The *breadth* of the love of God is what concerns the anxious sinner. The question of his heart is, " Will it admit me ? " And the blessed answer remains for ever, " God so loved the *world*, that He gave His only-begotten Son." " By me, if *any man* enter in, he shall be saved." When God says, " Whosoever will, may come," He means it ; and when the Apostle declares that God " will have all men to be saved," there can be no doubt whatever about the width of the gate..

The way in which some preachers talk about election is enough to frighten any convicted sinner. Thank God for election : it has its ordered place in the divinely-formed chain of truth, and there it yields its peculiar blessing and comfort, to the saint within the sanctuary of God. But it is not the message of God to the sinner. " Chosen in Him before the foundation of the world " is part of the heritage of the family within the house of God ; but the inscription on the outer gate, beaming before the needy sinner, in clear, bold letters, is, " WHOSOEVER WILL, MAY COME." The sinner who comes to God through Christ may rest assured that he will find a hearty welcome. The question of election will not be raised, but, like the prodigal of old, the kiss, the robe, the ring, shall all be his. Should the sinner refuse to enter by God's appointed way, he will never be able to find a defence by saying that there was no salvation for him ; nor will it be possible for one of the lost in the ever-burning lake to say, " I am here because

I was not elected to accept salvation." Ah no ; the door is wide enough for all. No one ever found it too narrow who came. The lament of Jesus is, "Ye will *not come* to Me that ye might have life."

Some might say, " I am too vile—I am too bad to enter." Ah, sinner, that gate was not for good people. It was for the transgressor. The Gospel is God's good news to the guilty. The salvation of God is for the lost. Pass in, then, guilty sinner, within the open gate. Your guilt is your passport : God's invitation is the assurance of your welcome. Heed not the giddy and the scoffing crowd who seek to turn you aside from God's appointed way, by telling you that no one can be sure of salvation now. Close your ears to all the conflicting sounds of earth, to all the sophistries of men, and hearken to the voice of Jesus, " I am the Door ; by ME if any man enter in, he SHALL BE SAVED." " *Shall be saved* " is the word. There is no doubt, no uncertainty about it. Thousands have entered, and they have been saved. They beckon you to enter in.

It was only one step. One moment the transgressor was outside the gate, the linen curtain *against* him, keeping him *out*. The next moment he was inside, the curtain was *for* him, surrounding him on every side and keeping him *in*. The reception of salvation is not a tedious process : it is not the work of months or years. It is done in a moment. That moment is when the sinner has done with himself and receives Christ, when he ceases to expect admission to God through His own righteousness, and enters in by Christ alone. God is pledged to save that sinner, and He does so at once and for ever. How wondrous is the transition ! From death to life—from darkness to light—from Satan to God ! The saved one stands within the circle of God's favour. He is no more an enemy, but a son. The linen curtain that once shut him out now shuts

him in ; he stands in grace, and righteousness is on his
side. He sees how the curtain hangs on the silver and is
upheld by the pillars in the sockets of copper. He learns
that God has saved him in righteousness through the
redemption of Christ and the judgment of sin.   How
secure and peaceful ! How safe and satisfied ! Sinner,
will you enter in before it be too late ? Will you pass in
within that open gate, to-day ?

> " Ere night that gate may close, and seal thy doom,
>   Then the last low, long cry, ' no room,' ' no room ' ;
>   O, woeful cry, ' no room ! ' " "

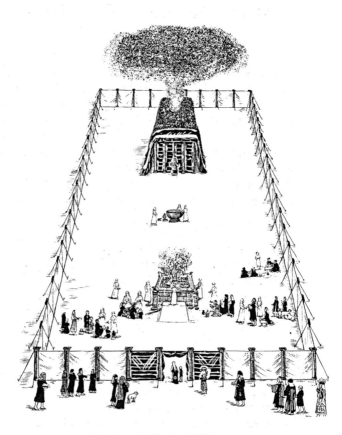

Tabernacle in the Wilderness

ALTAR OF BURNT OFFERING

(Exodus 27:1-8)

The two vessels that stood within the court of the
Tabernacle were the altar of burnt-offering and the brazen
laver. They stood in a straight line between the gate of
the court and the door of the Holy Place. In many points
they may be contrasted with all the other vessels. They
stood in the open court, visible to all the tribes ; the
services at both were of a public character. In this they
differ from the vessels of the Holy Place, which were seen
only by the priests who entered there. They were made of
copper, or shittim wood and copper ; whereas the inner
vessels were of gold, or shittim wood and gold. *Copper*
speaks to us of God in judgment ; *gold*, of God in glory.
Outside it is God in righteousness dealing with sin and
uncleanness : inside it is God revealed in His Divine
glory to His saints in communion with Himself.

Speaking broadly, the vessels *without* are typical of
Christ as He was down here, and of the work accomplished
by Him on earth and its application ; those *within*, of
Christ risen and glorified in the heavens, and of His work
continuously carried on up there for His saints. We need
both. Apart from the altar and laver no priest could ever
have entered the dwelling-place of God ; apart from the
golden altar no priest could have continued there. In the
brazen altar we see Christ meeting man's needs and
bringing the believer into abiding relationship with God.
In the golden altar we see Christ maintaining His saints

in conscious nearness and communion in that relationship. The altar in the court was the place of sacrifice. Our word altar, comes from a word that means " to kill "—a slaughter place. Ritualism with its altar in the Church is virtually a denial of the Cross and of the sufficiency of the sacrifice of Christ. It is " *the* altar "   (Exodus 29:12 ; 30:20), for there was no other. Christ, and Christ alone, is the answer to this type. He is " *the* altar " and " *the* Lamb." There is no other meeting-place between God and the sinner ; " there remaineth no more sacrifice for sin."

It is " the altar *at the door* " (Lev. 4:7), because there was no way of approach to God but by passing that altar ; there was no access to God but on the ground of sacrifice. Sinner ! let the full weight of this solemn truth fall upon your conscience. There is no way to God but by the blood of Christ. There, at the gate of the court, stood the transgressor yonder, at the western end, Jehovah of Israel sat upon His throne ; blood and water stood between. They tell out the need of atonement and cleansing ere the sinner can come nigh to God. The bright flame of fire, burning night and day upon the altar (Lev. 4: 12, 13) was the first sight that met the sinner's gaze as he cast his eyes towards the dwelling-place of God. The altar must be satisfied, its claims all met in full, before he could advance one step on his way to God. Fix your eyes, then, sinner, on that altar and its flame. It tells you of the God with whom you have to do, for " our God is a consuming fire " : not altogether love and mercy, as you are accustomed to think, but "glorious in holiness" as well. This was seen at " the place called Calvary," of which this altar speaks. The fire once kindled there, is surely enough to convince you that God can by no means clear the guilty. The judgment of sin, as seen in the Cross of Christ, is the ever-abiding witness that " the wages of sin is death." The fire was never to go out. So long as the holiness of God continues, so shall the punishment of sin. The unquenchable flame of that " eternal fire " in which the Christless one must for ever dwell, is an awful witness to the abiding holiness of God.

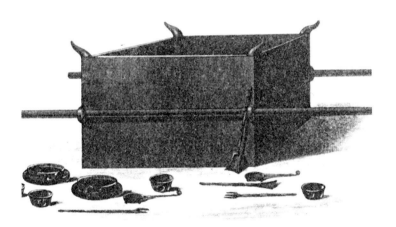

The Altar of Burnt Offering or Brazen Altar

The altar was four-square—the same on all sides. This signifies completeness—equality. " There is no difference " ; sinners of all ranks and conditions are equally needy, and no matter from where they come, Christ is the same for all. *It stood on the ground.* It was equally accessible to the child and the full-grown man. Such is the

Cross of Christ. It is within the sinner's reach, whatever may be his state ; no steps are required to reach it.

It was made of shittim wood and copper. Shittim wood alone could not have endured the fire ; the copper gave endurance and strength. " Shittim " or " incorruptible wood " is typical of the *humanity* of our Lord, and the copper in combination with it here, of the all-enduring strength of Jesus as " the Mighty God." What mysteries and combinations are here ! How our hearts should bow and our feet tread softly as we draw near to gaze on the *Person* of our glorious *Immanuel* ! He was as truly " the Virgin's child," the " Seed of the woman " who was to bruise the serpent's head, as He was " the Son " from the bosom of the Father. His manhood was perfect, as was His divinity. He was " Son of Man " and " Son of God." People sometimes say : " He took upon Him our sinful nature." But this is not the language of Holy Scripture, and the thought is deeply derogatory to the Person of our adorable Lord. I do not say that all who use such words are culpably guilty of this—I am sure that the very opposite is the case with many, and that they truly love the Lord. But we need in this, as in all the things of God, to rein in our own imaginations and avoid using proverbial expressions handed down from our fathers, holding fast and using the words of the Holy Ghost. *We* " were by nature the children of wrath," *we* were conceived in sin and shapen in iniquity ; the nature that *we* brought into the world with us was " enmity against God " in its very essence, and will continue to be so. It was not so with our blessed Lord. He was perfect in His manhood : there was no taint of fallen humanity in Him. His conception was by the power of the Holy Ghost ; He was " that Holy Thing " (Luke 1:35), the "Holy Child" (Acts 4:27), the "Holy One " (Acts 13:35). His flesh " saw no corruption " : it was the antitype of the " incorruptible wood."

The *horns* of the altar were on four corners. The horn in Scripture is often used to denote power (see Daniel 8: 3-20 ; Rev. 17:12). The horns of this altar were possibly used in binding the victim when it was presented alive before Jehovah—" Bind the sacrifice with cords to the altar's horns " (Psalm 118:27). They were sprinkled with the blood of atonement (Exodus 29:12), and there the guilty fled for refuge (1 Kings 2:28). The sinner who flees to Christ for refuge will prove the power of God in his immediate salvation. The moment he, by faith, lays hold of the blood, Almighty power is on his side, and will henceforth be his " horn of salvation " and " high tower " (Psalm 18:2), defending and upholding him.

In the *midst* of the altar was a network of copper : it would thus be one-and-a-half cubits high—the same height as the Mercy seat. We hear a great deal about the mercy of God, very little about His justice ; but the mercy of God and His justice are of the same dimensions, and His saints can say : " I will sing of *mercy* and *judgment* : unto Thee O God, will I sing ! " (Psalm 101:1).

On this network the burnt-offering was laid, and there consumed. The ashes fell through the network underneath, and were afterwards removed by the priest. How vividly all this pointed onward to the Cross of Christ. At early morn you might have seen the offerer moving on with his living victim toward the altar of God. He passed through the gate and stood beside the burning flame. There the victim was slain and flayed ; its various parts were all spread out, then raised upon the copper network, and from thence it ascended a sweet savour unto the Lord. A few hours later you might have seen a man clothed in pure linen garments coming from the altar with a copper pan filled with ashes in his hand. The victim had been offered and accepted, and the precious ashes were treasured up in a clean place without the camp.

We all remember what is written of that day on which the Lamb of God was sacrificed on a cross outside the gates of Jerusalem. It was a busy day, and the city was early astir. At early morn, priests were consulting and the multitude gathering. Later on, amid the stifled sobs of those who loved Him and the rage of His foes, the Lamb of God was led silently along the streets of Jerusalem and onward to the cross. Bound to the horns of the altar by the cords of love, He willingly died. The fire consumed the sacrifice. O! how precious in the sight of God was the lifeless form that hung upon that tree! How unspeakably dear the precious ashes of that whole burnt-offering! No rude hand of man was allowed to touch or break a bone of God's Holy Lamb. As the shades of evening fell, Joseph of Arimathea, His own disciple, came, bearing the body of the Lord wrapped in a clean linen cloth, and laid it in a clean new tomb, where no corrupting flesh of man had ever lain. The work was finished, the sacrifice was accepted, and the God of resurrection entered that rock-hewn tomb and raised Him from the dead. This is the Gospel of salvation for the sinner ; this is the mighty lever that raises him from the horrible pit and sets him among princes. Jesus died : He was buried : God raised Him from the dead. Glorious message! Blessed tidings! " IT IS FINISHED." We Sing—

> " No blood, no altar now,
> The sacrifice is o'er ;
> No flame, no smoke ascends on high,
> The lamb is slain no more."

THE OFFERINGS

Leviticus is the great book of sacrifice in the Old Testament; it may be studied along with the Epistle to the Hebrews, which is its counterpart in the New Testament. In the early part of that book we have five distinct offerings presented to us : the burnt-offering, the meat offering, the peace-offering, the sin-offering, and the trespass-offering. Viewed together, they present to us in type the one perfect offering of Christ ; viewed separately they present five different aspects of that one offering, as meeting the various needs of the people of God, in their access to God, their communion, and their worship.

It was after the children of Israel had left the land of Egypt, and become a people separated unto God, that this book was given to them. They had been brought into the wilderness to be alone with God, that He might instruct them in things concerning His worship and His service. It was there, in the waste, howling desert, that the mystic tent was set up and filled with glory ; it was there that the redeemed of the Lord began to learn practically their own imperfections and failures and the varied provisions of God's grace, as seen in the sacrifices and the priesthood. Those of the people of God who choose to linger in an Egypt-world, and whose lives are spent in conformity to its ways, know little experimentally of true communion and worship. They will not therefore readily apprehend those aspects of the work of Christ which maintain the saint in nearness to God. Their spiritual sensibilities are so blunted by the effects of worldliness, that shortcomings and failures do not appear

to be so hideous in their eyes as to drive them daily to
seek the repose of their souls in the varied excellences of
Christ's sacrifice. But the child of God who seeks to
walk along the desert in the company of His Father will
appreciate their value, at least in measure, and, as he
learns his own poverty and insufficiency, he will rejoice in
the riches and perfections of these offerings. It is a blessed
fact that, whether his intelligence in these things be small
or great, every believer in Christ Jesus stands accepted in
all the value that *God* has put upon the person and work
of His beloved Son. The new-born babe and the father
in Christ are alike in this : they stand upon the same
immovable rock : their title to the presence of God is
found in the same most precious blood ; they are " accepted " in the same " Beloved " ; but the peace and joy of the
soul, the strength and growth of spiritual life, depend
greatly on our apprehension and enjoyment of these things.

The offerings are divided into two classes, viz :—
sweet savour offerings and offerings for sin. The burnt-
offering, the meat-offering, and the peace-offering are in
the former class ; the sin and trespass-offerings in the
latter.

The order in which they are given to us in the Book
of Leviticus is, first, the burnt-offering, and last, the
sin and trespass-offerings. God *begins* by telling out to us
in type, the portion that *He* has found in the sacrifice of
Christ, and then that which meets our need. But the order
in which they were offered was the opposite of this, as,
for example, in the cleansing of the leper   (Lev. 14:12, 13),
and the consecration of the priesthood   (Lev. 8:14, 18).
And this is the order in which our souls apprehend the
varied riches of the One sacrifice of Jesus Christ. We
know Him *first* as the One who " died for our sins," then
as the One who gave Himself wholly to God for the lack
of devotedness in us. There can be no communion, no

worship, until sin has been disposed of and the conscience set at rest. It is only as we know our own deep need that we do in any measure apprehend the riches and sufficiency of the Perfect Sacrifice.

I have said that the offerings were divided into two classes, viz.: sweet savour offerings and offerings for sin. The sin and trespass-offerings are of this latter class. The distinctive features of these offerings are, that they were offered either for sins committed knowingly, or in ignorance ; that they were *not* burnt upon the altar in the Court, but carried forth without the camp and *burnt up* in the devouring fire as accursed of God. The victim was charged with the sin of the offerer, and its life was taken in his stead. Taken together, they point onward to Jesus as the bearer of sin and the curse ; they present to us in type His death, as meeting all the requirements of Divine justice for the sinner. He it was who " was made *sin* for us " (2 Cor. 5:21), and " who suffered for *sins*, the Just for the unjust, that He might bring us to God " (1 Peter 3:18). By His one perfect offering, the sins of all who believe are once and for ever put away, to be remembered again no more. The voice that speaks to us from the throne of God, in virtue of the death of Christ as our sin and trespass-offering, says : " Thine *iniquity* is taken away, and thy *sin* purged " ; " Their *sins* and *iniquities* will I remember no more " ; " Blessed is he whose *transgression* is forgiven, whose *sin* is covered."

THE TRESPASS-OFFERING was to make atonement for sins knowingly committed (Lev. 6:1, 7). It was offered for certain evil acts done against God and man ; it was not so much the guilty person as the evil deed that was prominent in this offering. This is generally the first thing that troubles the sinner when the Spirit of God begins to deal with him. He remembers the sins of his past life, he knows that the justice of God demands their punishment, and he

trembles at the prospect of meeting the Holy Judge.
How blessed to the troubled and awakened soul are the
tidings that Jesus has been our trespass-offering, that
" He was wounded for our transgressions, and bruised for
our iniquities," and that what we could not make resti-
tution of, to God or man—for we had " nothing to pay "
—our blessed Lord in His death has most fully done.
How sweet was the moment when we first beheld the
Lamb of God, and saw " ALL TRESPASSES " forgiven
(Col. 2:13).   It was then that we could take up the language
of the saint, and sing—

> " Here we find the dawn of Heaven,
>   While upon the Cross we gaze,
>   See our *trespasses* forgiven,
>   And our songs of triumph raise."

And ever since we have been converted (for the application
of these offerings is especially to the saints), how often have
our souls rejoiced in Jesus as our Trespass-offering ? We
have over and over again been wanderers from our Father's
side, and that deliberately and knowingly. Where should
we have been but for the abiding efficacy of the great
trespass-offering, which, blessed be God, shall never lose
its power.

> " Till every ransomed saint of God
>   Be saved to sin no more ! "

As the young believer goes on walking in the ways of
the Lord, and as the light of the truth of God shines in
upon his inner being, he begins to find out that he has
not only committed evil deeds, but that he has within
him an evil and revolted heart, a corrupt and sinful nature,
utterly opposed to God. He finds that he has been ignorantly, as well as knowingly, going on in rebellion against
the Lord. Things which did not at first appear to him to

be sinful have, by the light of truth, been shown to be so,
and he now groans over the years of ignorant indulgence
of them. The provision of God's grace for this is the
SIN-OFFERING. It was not sin as *we* were acquainted with
it, nor sin as we were consciously and confessedly guilty
of it, that was laid upon the Lamb of God, in the day that
His soul was made an offering for sin, but SIN as it was
gauged by the Holy Judge ; SIN as it was known by Him
against whom it has been committed. The words " I lay
my sins on Jesus " are but the expression of an unscriptural
thought concerning sin. Our consciousness of sin may be
great or small, according to the measure of our light and
the sensitiveness of our consciences, but, blessed be the
God who loved us, that He charged *all* our sins upon the
great Sin-Offering, and put them all away for ever. Yea,
more ; He condemned *sin,* and set man aside, closing his
account for ever as a child of Adam at the Cross. How
blessed for the soul to grasp this precious truth ! That God
has dealt with sin, and settled every question regarding it
once and for all at the Cross, and that the abiding efficacy
of the blood remains before God most precious for ever.
Is this a license for the believer to sin ? God forbid !
Does this imply that he is to take no notice of sins committed
after conversion ? Most assuredly not. As a *child* of God,
confession and a Father's forgiveness will be daily needed.
If he goes on with sin unconfessed, his Father's faithful
hand will use the rod. But his account, as a man in the
flesh, as a child of Adam, a *sinner,* was finally closed and
" settled " at the Cross of Christ. As we grow in the knowledge of what *we are* and of what we have *done* (it may be
ignorantly), we shall be driven to seek the daily rest of our
souls in the perfectness of the great Sin-Offering.

Many are disposed to think and speak lightly of sins
committed in ignorance. If worthy of being reckoned sins
at all, they are, according to such, of comparatively small

account. But such thoughts are not the thoughts of God. " *If a soul sin . . . though he wist it not,* YET IS HE GUILTY " (Leviticus 5:17),is the irrevocable verdict of the Court of Heaven concerning sins of ignorance. Let's consider this. Ignorance is not innocence. It is frequently the result of a protracted course of rebellion against the light, and of playing fast and loose with the truth of God. The conscience becomes so seared, and the heart so hardened, that the most heinous sins may be committed ignorantly. Could anything be more awful than this ? How utterly gone from God must that man be who can sin against Him, and persecute His saints, and yet suppose he is doing God service ! The priests and rulers of Jerusalem condemned and crucified the Son of God, and yet they *knew not* what they did   (Luke 23:34).   Peter told them : " I wot that through *ignorance* ye did it " (Acts 3 : 17) ; but none will surely say they did no evil. Saul of Tarsus, while he persecuted the saints, believed he was serving God (1 Tim 1:13), but he tells us he did it " *ignorantly* in unbelief ". There are many around us whose minds are so blinded that they are scattering deadly error, and believe it to be the truth ; they are leading men to the lake of fire, yet sincerely suppose they will reach the City of God. But this is not confined to unregenerate sinners ; there are many of the professed children of God judicially blinded. They have trifled with the light that once shone upon them, until it has now become darkness. Truths once known but not obeyed have been torn from their grasp. Precepts and commands, long unheeded, have ceased to exercise their consciences. We constantly hear it said : " We can do so-and-so with a good conscience " ; but man's conscience is not the standard : it is, " What saith the Lord ! " A conscience not guided by Scripture is a terrible tool in Satan's hands. We have the *Book* containing the complete revelation of the will of God :

we are therefore responsible to know His will and to do it. When some fresh ray of light shines in upon our souls, when some long-held tradition is found out to be false, when some long-loved association is shown by the light of truth to be an " unequal yoke," a fellowship of darkness, and when through grace we renounce and forsake it, with sorrow that we had continued so long in what was so contrary to the will of God, we ought to confess our *sins* of *ignorance.* We shall then prove the grace of God and appreciate the sufficiency of Christ, as the One who became the Sin-Offering for these very sins committed ignorantly.

The sin-offering was to be " without blemish." Jesus was " the Lamb without blemish and without spot " (1 Peter 1:19). In Him was no sin. He " knew no sin " (2 Cor. 5:21). He "did no sin" (1 Peter 2:22). The sin-offering was " *most holy* " (Lev. 6:25). It was presented before the Lord, and the offerer identified himself with it. He " *leaned* " (as the word signifies) his hand upon its head as if he had said, " I take this spotless victim to be my substitute ; I lean my whole weight upon its merit." The offerer's sin was charged upon the victim, and it was killed before the Lord. Nothing short of death could satisfy the altar's claims ; but when the blood was poured at its base all its demands were met. The " wages of sin is death," and " Christ died for our sins, according to the Scriptures " (1 Cor. 15:3). This is the first note of the Gospel of God. Sinner, have you believed the message? To believe is to be forgiven ; to receive the testimony of God is to be eternally saved. The sacrifice has been offered and when by faith I lay my guilty hand upon His spotless head and say, " He gave Himself for me," I stand discharged before the Court of Heaven—justified by His blood.

The fat was burned upon the altar. This was Jehovah's

portion. The excellency of Jesus was fully appreciated
by His God when He stood as our substitute bearing sin.
Personally, He was ever well-pleasing to Him. For at no
time was Christ more entirely well-pleasing to His God
than when He offered Himself as a sacrifice for a " sweet-
smelling savour " (Eph. 5:2).

The victim was carried without the camp and burnt.
Jesus was cast out and forsaken of His God when our
sins were laid upon Him. It was then that the awful cry
came from his lips—" My God, My God, why hast Thou
forsaken Me ? " It was there that the devouring flame
consumed the sin-offering. For the believer it is quenched
for ever. The judgment of the believer is past ; there is
now no condemnation. Take your stand, ye doubting
saints, beside the altar of the Lord. See " the blood " and
the " fat," the life and the excellency of Jesus, given to
God for you. It is enough. Justice asks no more. The
righteous claims of God are satisfied. Then look at that
heap of ashes being scattered by the winds of heaven
outside the camp : they are the memorials of wrath
appeased and of sin put away. *Your sins are gone*—gone
to return no more. " It is God that justifieth ; who is he
that condemneth ? "

The burnt-offering, the meat-offering, and the peace-
offering are all " sweet savour " offerings. They were not
carried forth without the camp and burnt up in the
devouring fire, but either wholly burnt upon the altar, or
shared by the offerer and the priest.

THE BURNT-OFFERING is sometimes called the " ascend-
ing offering," because the word translated " burnt-
offering " is " *holah*," and means " that which ascends."
It was Jehovah's portion ; it was wholly burnt upon the
altar ; it all ascended up to Jehovah in sweet fragrance,
affording Him satisfaction and delight.

The distinctive feature in the burnt-offering is, that it

was wholly for Jehovah. The offerer presented something to Him that gratified His heart, and in which he found delight. When the offerer brought his sin-offering the language of his heart was, " I have sinned against the Lord " ; " I have done that which He commanded me not to do." He came to God as the Judge of sin, bringing an offering to appease His wrath. When he brought his burnt-offering to the altar he came bringing an offering for " His acceptance " (as Lev. 1:3 ought to read). It was something of value, giving pleasure and delight to Jehovah's heart, which he personally could not give. The burnt-offering presents to us in type the *unreserved devotedness of the Lord Jesus ; His perfect surrender to God in life and in death.* " He offered Himself without spot *to God* " (Heb. 9:14). " He gave Himself *for us* an offering and a sacrifice to God of a sweet-smelling savour " (Eph. 5:2). All that He was, He was unto God, and " *for us.*"

The burnt-offering was all for Jehovah, yet it was offered for the offerer's acceptance with Him.

The offerer stood with his hand upon the victim's head as if he had said, " I have no devotedness, no preciousness, but I present this perfect offering for my acceptance before the Lord." Thus he stood identified with, and accepted in, his offering. The whole of its value became his own, the moment his hand was laid upon its head. It ceased that moment to be a question of what *he* was, and became a question of what *his offering* was. Will IT give satisfaction ? Will IT be accepted by Jehovah ?

How blessed it is for the soul to get a grasp of all this ! To the believer in Christ it is no longer " Just as *I* am," but " Just as THOU art." His own identity as a sinner is lost ; he ceases to be reckoned as a child of Adam before God ; his own worthless self is blotted out ; and he stands identified with Christ henceforth and for ever. The value, the preciousness, the beauty of the Son of God, are reckoned to be his own. He stands before God "in Christ," accepted in his Representative. May the Holy Ghost make this plain to you, beloved friends. I know that I cannot do it, but if He, the Spirit of Truth, do but bring it home to your souls in power, it will make you leap for very joy. It will dispel the fear and dark forebodings that hover around the soul, as mists and storm-clouds flee before the rising sun. Some of you, I know, have times of despondency and fear. You lose your peace and joy, and get away back to "Doubting Castle," to be under the power of "Giant Despair." Then your souls go groping in the dark, and sighing—

> "Do I love the Lord or no,
> Am I His or am I not?"

Your own unworthiness becomes the doleful dirge of your soul, and the memory of your lack of devotedness and faithfulness to God almost brings you to despair. Now I would not have you suppose that we ought to look upon these things lightly. I am sure that to learn one's own unworthiness is a wholesome and necessary lesson. To know by painful experience that we have not loved the Lord with heart and soul and strength and mind, as He commands, is painful knowledge to a truly quickened soul; but alongside this, I desire that we may see what God has done *for us, where* He has put us, and what *He* there esteems us to be.

This is the lesson of the burnt-offering. The offerer came, conscious of his own unworthiness, to offer a victim in his stead. It was killed before the Lord. Its life was taken instead of his. Then it was flayed and divided. Its various parts were exposed to the light; it was shown to be both inwardly and outwardly perfect. Then it was all raised upon the altar, and from the copper grating upon which it lay the *whole* went up—a sweet savour (or, "a savour of rest ")—unto Jehovah, and the offerer was accepted according to the value of the offering. How sweetly does all this speak to us of Jesus. God has fulfilled the word uttered on Mount Moriah long ago, and " provided Himself a Lamb for a burnt-offering " (Gen. 22). He found Him in His own bosom, the beloved of His heart. How dear, how precious to His Father no human heart can conceive, no tongue can tell. But we do know this, and it is our deepest joy, that *the Father* has fully estimated His worth and appreciated His excellency, and we are accepted according to the measure of the Father's delight in Him.

" There came a fire out from before the Lord and consumed upon the altar the burnt-offering and the fat " (Lev. 9:24). This was the witness of its acceptance (see Ps. 20:3). The burning of the offering here and the burning of the sin-offering outside the camp are very different. *Here* it is the holy altar-fire feeding on a victim well-pleasing to Jehovah ; *there* it is the judgment-fire devouring a victim accursed because of sin. Indeed, a different Hebrew word is used. The word " burn," used in connection with the burnt-offering, means " *to burn as incense* " (see Lev. 1: 9, 13, 15, 17) ; but the word used in connection with the sin-offering, means " *to burn up* or consume in a devouring fire " ; (for its use see Lev. 4: 12 ; 6:30 ; Josh. 7:15). The Lord Jesus in His death had to do with both. *Personally*, He was the Holy One offered up " without spot to God," and the fragrance of His offering went up as an incense. *Representatively*, " He was made sin " and a " curse " for us (2 Cor. 5:21 ; Gal. 3:13). The whole of the offering was consumed. The head and the fat, the inwards and the legs, were all reduced to ashes. Jehovah got all ; nothing remained. How true was this of Jesus. His thoughts, His hidden energies, His affections, and His ways were wholly devoted to God. Of Him, and Him only, can it be said that " He loved the Lord His God with *all* His heart, and *all* His soul, and *all* His strength, and *all* His mind," and this He did continuously and perfectly. If He thought, it was for God ; if He preached or healed, it was not only for men's blessing, but for God's glory. His time and His strength were all spent for God alone. His own ease and comfort, His own loss or gain, never had a thought. Whether on the mountain all night in prayer, or asleep on a pillow in a boat, all was for His God. He " set the Lord always " before Him, and He " always did those things that pleased " His Father. O that men who lightly speak or sing of being " wholly consecrated to God " and " having their all upon the altar " would here see what it means. Jesus is the standard and the measure of " complete surrender unto God." Every other standard is a counterfeit and a fallacy.

To His worth the Father bore witness both in His life and death. When He stood in the Jordan at His baptism and on the holy mount at His transfiguration, the Father's voice was heard saying, " This is My beloved Son, in whom I am well pleased." All that He was and all that He is, is *for* us. He stands the Representative of all His people. They are all viewed as *in* Him, adorned with His beauty. The voice from Heaven to us is, that we are " ACCEPTED in the *Beloved* " (Eph. 1:6), and that " the Lord TAKETH PLEASURE in His people " (Ps. 149:4). Think of this, ye doubting, downcast saints : " *Accepted* " —not in *your* love or *your* faithfulness—but in " THE BELOVED " : In Him who is the Father's delight. Accepted —according to the measure of the Father's delight—in His own beloved Son. This is the inalienable standing of the saints of God. The weakest babe in Christ is adorned in His beauty, is a possessor of His life, and is loved as He is loved. We may all take up the language of the hymn—

" The love wherewith He loves the Son
Such is His love to me."

Do you really believe it, beloved? Have you in your heart said " amen " to it, and do you enjoy its bliss from day to day? There is no " higher life " than this. This is the highest and best, and it is the normal position of all the saints : the birthright and portion of all the family of God. We must believe it to enjoy it. Put down your foot firmly, then, on the word—" Accepted in the Beloved." Make it your own. Like the negro, of whom some of you have read, said, "I am poor, and black, and vile, but in Christ Jesus I am *holy*, and *pure*, and *fair*, just BECAUSE I'M IN HIM."

THE MEAT OR MEAL-OFFERING, presents to us the *perfectness of the Human life of the Lord Jesus, ending in death* : the perfectness of His character as Man, manifested in His life down here. It was a sweet savour unto God ; it was the food of the priest.

It was made of " *fine flour.*" Flour that had no need of bruising or sifting ; no roughness or uneven-ness in it. This is an emblem of the human nature of the Lord. As a man He was perfect ; there was no fibre of the fallen nature of man in Him ; nothing that required to be subdued or kept under. Chastening and bruising are often needed to make us bow to the will of God. Not so our blessed Lord. His delight was to do His Father's will ; meekness and submissiveness were *naturally* His. And what He was, He always was. We are one day submissive, the next day fretful ; sometimes bold, then timid ; full of fervour and cold alternately. Our Lord was ever the same. His submission to the Father's will was as manifest in the garden as on the hill of glory. His gentleness was not more apparent when the little child lay in His arms than when His foes surrounded Him in the judgment hall.

Oil was poured upon it. Oil is the emblem of the Holy Spirit (see 1 John 2:27 ; 2 Cor. 1:21:23).

Jesus was " anointed with the Holy Ghost and power " (Acts 10:38). All that He did was in the power of the Spirit. His rebukes and His consolations, His service and His sufferings, were *all* in the Spirit of God. He lived and walked, and, through the eternal Spirit, " offered Himself without spot to God " (Heb. 9:14).

Frankincense was put upon it. This is the type of purity and fragrance. The more it comes in contact with the fire, its fragrance is increased. We know it was so with Jesus. His sorrows and deprivations, and especially His sufferings on the cross, brought out the fragrance of His character and manifested His moral glory.

" Ye shall burn *no leaven.*" Leaven is a corrupting thing, and always used in Scripture as the emblem of evil. There was none of this evil principle in Jesus, His flesh saw no corruption.

" Neither any *honey.*" If leaven be the emblem of the sourness and corruption of man's nature, honey is the emblem of its sweetness. It is one of the sweetest things of earth, but it very soon corrupts and becomes sour. It will not stand the fire. There was none of this in Jesus. His love was not mere natural affection which is easily cooled. It stood the test because it was the Love Divine, love that could stoop to wash the feet of one who was to deny Him, and of others who were to forsake Him. How much of that which passes current among the saints as love, turns out in the hour of trial to be fermenting honey. It is mere natural sweetness, and when crossed or slighted, it turns to sourness. Friendships and fellowships based upon this effervescent kind of love, fade and fail. Love that details no faithful wounds is not the love of Jesus. But love that cleaves to its object, through good and evil report, rebuking and correcting it, studying not its own pleasure but the loved one's profit, is after the manner of the love of Christ to us.

Salt was the next ingredient. It is preservative in its nature. " Let your speech be always with grace seasoned with salt " (Col. 4:6) This element was ever manifested in the Lord. " The salt of the covenant of His God " was never lacking in His dealings with man. In faithful love He rebuked Martha and Peter among His own, and He denounced the hollow religion of the Pharisees to their very face. He was " full of grace," but it never degenerated into softness, nor His rebukes into harshness.

THE PEACE-OFFERING.—The distinguishing feature of this offering is, that Jehovah, the priest, and the offerer have all a portion in it. In this it differs from the burnt-offering. *There*, it was Jehovah receiving His portion ; the whole of it was consumed upon the altar. *Here*, it is Jehovah satisfied, having received His portion, and now ministering to His people. It is pre-eminently the *communion* offering. Communion with God, and with one another, are typified here. To feed at the same table, to share the same portion, is the expressive type of communion. And wondrous as the privilege may seem, yet it is nevertheless true, that *we* have been called to the fellowship of the Father and His Son Jesus Christ. *Less* than this could not have satisfied the love of the Father's heart, *more* than this He could not give. Like the prodigal of old, we have been welcomed to His heart, and seated with Him at His table, and all this in perfect righteousness, and therefore in perfect peace. It is of the very utmost importance that our souls should clearly apprehend the basis of this peace and communion and what is necessary for their enjoyment. " Peace with God " is not an unstable, flickering experience, flowing from some spiritual attainment or inward sanctity. It is an unchangeable reality, fruit of the finished work of Christ. Every charge that law and justice had against us

He met, and every lacking virtue He supplied, when He offered Himself to God for us. We see this in the peace-offering. It tells us of the *inward perfectness of the Lord Jesus*, presented to God for us.

The fat was all burned upon the altar. It was Jehovah's portion. As *all* the " frankincense " of the meat-offering was for Him, so was *all* the " fat " of the peace-offering. There were hidden and inward excellences in the Lord Jesus that none on earth could value or appreciate. They were exclusively Jehovah's portion. The depth of the devotedness and the strength of the love that dwelt within His holy soul none could fathom save His Father, for " no man knoweth the Son, but the Father." Blessed to know that He has fully valued and appreciated His excellency, and we are accepted before God in the full value thereof.

The *kidneys* were also offered. They typify the seat of the inward condition. The word is sometimes translated " reins." None but the Lord Jesus could invite the searching eye of Him who saith : " I the Lord search the *heart* ; I try the *reins* " to scan His inward parts. He only could say, " Examine Me, O Lord, and prove Me ; try My *reins* and My *heart* " (Psalm 26:2) ;   and when He was tried and proved by the deep suffering of the cross, He was found to be perfect *inwardly* as well as *outwardly*. With us it is not so. Our inward being is not fit for the altar of God even after we have been " born again " and made partakers of the " Divine nature." Who is there among us but knows that the carnal mind—the old man— is still there as well ? And this would of itself mar and disturb our peace and communion with God, even were this evil principle never to bear its fruits in the form of active sin. The presence of evil there would be unbearable to a soul knowing the nature and character of God but for the virtues of the great peace-offering. But, blessed be

God that in the riches of His grace He has given us to know that our worthless, sinful selves are *blotted out* and *buried out of His sight*, and that the sin that dwells within us is *covered* by the efficacy of the sacrifice of Christ, thus enabling us to commune with God in peace, in spite of all that we feel and see ourselves to be. We walk with God in the light, not because we never sinned, or have no sin in us, but because " the blood of Jesus Christ, His Son, cleanseth us from all sin." Our feet stand upon redemption ground ; our peace is made eternally secure through the blood of His cross. The efficacy of that one sacrifice abides before God for ever, and for us. God is satisfied in Christ. So are we. This is communion.

It is not our sanctity of heart or our spiritual attainments that are the ground of peace ; nor is it the work of the Holy Spirit within us. These are all fluctuating and imperfect as regards their measure. The ground of peace is the FINISHED and PERFECTED work of Christ *for us*. That is what we find typified in the peace-offering.

It was killed before the Lord. The blood was sprinkled upon the altar, and the *fat* and *inwards* were burned for a sweet savour. The *life* and inward excellencies were the portion of Jehovah ; He received His portion first, then the offerer and the priest each received their portion. God being satisfied, a table was spread for man, and furnished with part of the sacrifice already presented on the altar. The *altar* is the place of offering towards God. The *table*, the place of God's ministering towards His people. Such is the relation of the Lord's Supper to the Cross. Apart from the cross, there could have been no table. It is the memorial of what was accomplished at the cross, and the expression of the believer's fellowship in it. How daring an insult to God and to His Christ it is, to erect an *altar* in the church, with man-made *priests* offering *sacrifice* for the living and the dead around it. It is a subversion of the very foundations of the faith, and a flat denial of the finished work of Christ. At the table we have fellowship with God in peace, over His beloved Son, and we have fellowship one with another. What a sight! Every eye is fixed on Christ; every heart is satisfied. The Father alone can rightly esteem the inward preciousness and devotedness of His own Beloved, but we as priests can rejoice as we feed on the "wave breast" and "heave shoulder"—the symbols of His *love and power*. How tender a pillow is His bosom for the weary head! How strong is His mighty shoulder, for the weak and fainting soul!

We have now briefly sketched the varied offerings and sought to glean a few of their simplest teachings, but "the half hath not been told." When we stand before His glorious throne, perfectly conformed to His image, the last trace of sin and fallen humanity gone and forgotten, then—but not till then—shall we *fully* know the preciousness and worth of the PERFECT SACRIFICE—THE GREAT PEACE-OFFERING.

THE LAVER

The Laver was the second vessel in the Court of the Tabernacle. It stood between the altar of burnt-offering and the Holy Place. We are not told the shape or size of this vessel, nor do we find any account of how it was carried along the desert. These are among " the secret things that belong unto the Lord," and we must not guess, or seek to be wise above that which is written. The silence of the Scriptures in points such as these is as significant as it is Divine : there is no overlook, no forget-fulness on the part of the writer. The other vessels are all described minutely in their length and breadth, as also the bars and rings by which they were lifted from off the earth and borne upon the Levites' shoulders during the march (see Num. 4).   But in the instructions concerning the laver there is no command concerning rings or staves. Is this an overlook ? No, surely.

It had a *foot* of copper. In this it differed from all the other vessels. The bars and rings by which they were raised up to be carried seem to indicate that, although they stood *upon* the earth, yet they were not *of* it, but belonged to Heaven. They were shadows of heavenly things, the enduring substance of which has its place in the heavenly sanctuary. The laver having a foot connecting it *with,* yet raising it *above* the earth, may show that the line of spiritual teaching in this vessel is connected with the *earthly life* and *walk* of a people whose birth and citizen-ship is from Heaven. The present world is the sphere where the hands and the feet of God's redeemed require the use of the laver ; it is only *down here,* amid the defilements and pollutions of earth, that its gracious ministry is needed, for once *up there*, the feet of the saints can contract no defilement. The street of gold, like unto transparent glass upon which they stand, shall for ever reflect their purity. Corresponding with this, we have in the Book of Revelation—itself a book of signs and symbols —allusion made to all the furniture of the Temple or Tabernacle, but there is no mention made of the laver or brazen sea. In striking contrast, we behold there a sea of glass reflecting the chaste beauty of the redeemed. The last stain has been washed from off the feet ; earth's sands defile no more ; the saints are glorified in the image of their Lord, and the laver and brazen sea are no longer needed. Blessed future ! Holy, happy prospect of the child of God !

It was made from the brazen looking-glasses of the women of Israel (Exodus 38:8). The looking-glass reflects one's self. It shows the beauties or deformities of the person, but cannot alter either. It reveals defilement, but cannot take it away. The woman's beauty is her distinctive mark ; she would therefore naturally value that which shows it, but the mirrors were gladly given up to make a laver for the priests of God. This was a precious fruit of grace. Have you ever given up anything for God, dear fellow-saints ? Has the grace of God got such a hold of your heart that things once too fondly loved have been surrendered to Jesus ? There are many who profess to admire the " beauty of the Lord," and to esteem the " Man of Sorrows " to be the " Altogether Lovely," who yet adorn themselves in the grandeur of the earth, and seek to be well thought of, in the world that rejected and cast out their Lord. Such have never yet really seen the " present evil age " and the " end of all flesh " from God's standpoint ; they view themselves in their own mirrors, and think and speak well of themselves. But the thoughts of man are not the thoughts of God ; therefore we must surrender all our own ideas and fancies, and submit ourselves to the judgment of the Lord. The moment we do so, accepting His verdict and sentence, we learn how God in grace has provided that which cleanses us from spiritual defilement and that fits us for His Holy Temple.

The laver was filled with water, and thereat the priests washed their hands and feet as they went into the Holy Place to worship and as they came out to the altar to serve. The neglect of this was death. There was no worship conducted at this vessel—there was no blood-shedding connected with it—and yet there could have been no worship, true, no service, without its use. It was the daily need of the priests ; by its use they were kept in a condition of cleanness, in which they could exercise the functions of their priestly office before the Lord and toward His people. How infinitely precious are the lessons to be learned by us at the side of the laver ; how practical and searching are the truths conveyed to us in this expressive type ! May the Holy Spirit guide us into the truth, and give us honest hearts and tender consciences, while it searches us as with a lighted candle. We have seen in the altar and its sacrifices the work of Christ accomplished *for* us, and our acceptance before God according to the value of that work. It is all *reckoned* or imputed to us the moment we believe, and this once for all. The believer is regarded as standing in Christ, *eternally* cleansed, *eternally* accepted, by virtue of the once-offered sacrifice. There is no repetition of this act, no " fresh application of the blood," as it is sometimes called. He is abidingly brought into a relationship with God, where he is regarded as " clean every whit," and " sanctified once for all " ; and all this is inalienably and eternally his, through a work accomplished *for* him by Another. The teaching of the laver is entirely different. It speaks of a work accomplished

in us by the *Word* and the *Spirit* of God. It goes on
continuously from day to day. There is no stage or condition of Christian life on earth where it can be said to be
completed. There is no possible state or experience
attainable here when a saint may do without this cleansing
at the laver, and it is truly sad that some should think
and speak as though it were otherwise.

There were two distinct washings of the priesthood.
In order to understand the teaching conveyed by the
laver it is necessary to remember this. The priests on
the day of their consecration were brought up to the door
of the Tabernacle and washed all over with water by Moses
(see Exodus 29:4 ; Lev. 8:6). This was the first act
in their consecration. No holy garment, no anointing oil
was put upon them until they were " washed," and not
till then were they allowed to pass within the Holy Place
to worship God. This washing was performed for them by
another ; they had no hand in it at all. Throughout the
entire period of their priesthood this act was never repeated.
This accords with the " laver of regeneration " (Titus 3:5,
R.V.). The word in Exodus 29:4, translated
" wash," signifies " to wash all over," and is different
from the word used in connection with the laver (Exod.
30:18). It is a washing that must take place before
the place of worship and service can be entered, and
having been once accomplished, the priest stands under
its abiding efficacy. It is so with the second birth, the
washing of regeneration. No man can worship God until
he has been born again ; he cannot enter the presence of
God to commune with Him until he has received a nature
that enables him to do so. Let this be clearly understood.
Man in his natural state can neither appreciate anything
that is of God nor do anything well-pleasing to Him. He
may be clever and intellectual, or even moral and religious,
but until he has been born from above, his place is outside

the circle of the family of God, and outside the circle of
the worship and service of the heavenly priesthood. He
dare not cross the threshold of the Holy Place, until by the
sovereign act of God's grace, he is pronounced " clean
every whit," his heart sprinkled from an evil conscience,
his body washed with pure water.

Here, in passing, let me ask you to pause and consider
whether this washing has ever taken place in your case ?
Has there been a moment in your life's history when you
were brought face to face with the living God and stripped
of all your fancied goodness. Have you, like Joshua the
high priest (Zech. 3), been stripped of the filthy rags of
your self-righteousness, and clothed in the " garments of
glory and beauty " of God's providing ? Have you ever
been truly brought to God—converted—born again ?
Whatever may be your position in the professing Church
on earth, let me solemnly assure you that, apart from this,
you will find no place in the Kingdom of God. Nicodemus
was brought up to the door of that Kingdom, and told by
the Son of God that unless he was " born again " he could
neither " see " nor " enter " it, and the words remain
unaltered for ever.

The priests once cleansed, and their consecration
completed, might enter the Holy Place ; indeed it was now
to be their home. Its boards enclosed them, its curtains
o'ershadowed them, they walked in the light of its candlestick, and fed on its bread. When they went forth to do
service for God, toward the leper or the unclean, it was as
those whose abiding place was in the covert of His Tabernacle. The place of the unclean was foreign to their nature,
their home was with God. O that it were always so with
us, beloved. When we go forth to preach the Gospel to
the sinner, do we go as priests in communion with God ?
When we go forth to seek to win an erring brother, do we
always go forth as from the Holy Place, in the power of

communion with God ? When we walk in the world do
we tread it as a strange country ? How true and real our
work for God would be if it were always so with us. What
an antidote to the busy, fruitless labour of the flesh is this
abiding in the presence of God. May we prove it so from
day to day.

The laver was placed between the altar and the door,
and the priests were commanded to wash their hands and
feet thereat. It was an easy matter for the once-cleansed
hands and feet to contract defilement. The hands constantly *working* in the service of God at the altar, the feet
ever *walking* on the desert sand, would be in continuous
need of washing, and for this the water in the laver was
given. No unclean priest was allowed to minister to the
Lord on penalty of death—for " Holiness becometh Thine
House, O Lord, for ever."

This is a solemn truth. It speaks to us of the *condition*
of soul necessary for those who worship and serve the
living God. One might be a priest and yet, because of
uncleanness upon him, become unfit to exercise the
functions of his priestly office. So may one who is truly a
child of God, but living in habitual neglect of God's Word,
or in unjudged, unconfessed sin, have no present communion with God, or ability to serve or worship Him.
The priest's title to enter was the *blood* of the sacrifice,
but the condition necessary for the using of that title was
that his hands and feet had been cleansed with *water*. This
bespeaks the title and condition necessary to communion
with God. Spiritual life is not all ; there must be a walk
in the light, self-judgment, and a continual testing and
cleansing of all our *works* and *ways* by the Word of God,
if we would walk with Him. The Word of God is the
means by which the Lord keeps His people clean and in
condition for communion and service. " By what means
shall a young man cleanse his way ? By taking heed

thereto, according to Thy word " (Psalm 119:9). " Sanctify them through Thy truth : *Thy Word* is truth " (John 17:17).

To neglect the judgment of our works and ways by the Word is to thwart the Lord's purpose in our sanctification and the purification of us as a peculiar people to Himself. In John 13 we see the Lord as the girded servant washing His disciples' feet—cleansing that from them which would have hindered them from having part *with* Him. Here we have the same lesson. He lives in Heaven above, our great High Priest ; His Word is with us here, to cleanse and keep us in communion with Him. When we come to that Word with honest hearts, prepared to do whatever it commands, and to renounce whatever it condemns, He applies it to us, and thus we are separated from every evil work and way, and cleansed from all unrighteousness. If we refuse to allow Him to separate evil from us, by the cleansing of the Word, He will tell us, as He did of old, " If I wash thee not, thou hast no part with Me," and thus it is that communion is broken ; the conscience becomes clogged, and an open fall ensues.

May it be our conscious experience, as it is our privilege, to walk daily in His light, saying, " Search me, O God, and know my heart ; try me and know my thoughts " (Psalm 139:23), and when He shows us some evil way, some defiling spot, may we at once submit our feet to Him and have it cleansed away.

The Brazen Laver

THE TABERNACLE

Sockets of Silver

We have now to consider the foundation and frame-work of the Tabernacle—the sockets of silver, the boards of shittim wood overlaid with gold, and the bars with their rings of gold ; or, in other words, the foundation, the walls, and that which bound the walls together.

We have formerly discussed that the Tabernacle was the first dwelling-place of God on this earth, and that it was typical of the Church, His present habitation among men. As the glory dwelt of old within the boards and curtains of that mystic tent in the wilderness, and nowhere else on earth, even so now is the presence of God known among those who " are builded together for an habitation of God through the Spirit " (Eph. 2:22). There was no Gentile temple, however gorgeous or magnificent, that could claim to be the dwelling-place of Jehovah of Israel. Their pomp and grandeur might attract the kings of the earth, and draw thousands to worship around their shrine, but the chosen habitation of the God of Heaven was an humble tent constructed according to His own pattern, and ordered according to His own will—the place where His authority was owned and His commands obeyed. We read concerning the building of it, that " behold they had done it *as* the Lord had commanded, *even so* had they done it " (Exodus 39:43) ; and the response of Jehovah to His people's obedience is recorded in the thrilling words—" So Moses finished the work. THEN a cloud covered the tent of the congregation, and the glory of the

Lord *filled* the Tabernacle " (Exodus 40:33, 34). Blessed, but solemn, is the lesson here taught us. The place where the presence and power of the Lord are manifested must be one of His own constructing and ordering. The traditions and will of man must have no place or authority there. Had there been a pin or bar needed, or a single knop or flower too many, I surely believe that the Lord would not have sanctioned the self-will or disobedience of the people by coming down to dwell in that Tabernacle. But everything was done according to His will, and He came down and took possession of His house with all His heart. The age in which we live is one of spiritual things ; the habitation of God is therefore " a spiritual house," and built of living stones (1 Peter 2:5). Such is the Church of the living God. It is composed of men and women who have life in Christ, and of no other. The unconverted have no place, no portion there. This is the first essential thing— that those who compose the building be living souls, all born from above. But this of itself is not enough. They must be builded together according to God's pattern. They must be gathered unto Christ, and according to the Word of God. The order of their worship, their ministry, and rule must be " as the Lord hath commanded," before they can expect or count upon the promised presence of the Lord, or be accounted His house. To be God's house, His habitation, His church, is much more than is often supposed. It is a *conditional* privilege, and may be forfeited (Heb. 3:6 ; Rev. 2:5), although the ultimate salvation of the individuals who compose it never can. Moreover, the introduction of false material, either in the case of false disciples or bad doctrine being brought into the building, will defile it and bring it under the present judgment of the Lord (1 Cor. 3:16, 17 ; 1 Peter 4:17). May our hearts and ways be so ordered before our God, beloved, that as individuals, He can come to dwell and walk with us, and then when we gather together unto His blessed Name, He may dwell and walk among us with complacency and joy.

We will now look at the foundation of silver. Each of the 48 boards stood upon two silver sockets. The shifting sand of the desert afforded no solid base on which to erect the shittim boards. They were built upon a foundation of God's own providing. It was both valuable and enduring. If we turn to Exodus 30:11-16 we shall see whence this silver came. It was the *atonement money* of the people. In the day of Israel's numbering, every man whose name went down in the Book of Numbers brought half a shekel of silver as a ransom for his soul. It mattered not of what tribe he was, or of what pedigree ; he might be able to tell out all this with perfect clearness, yet his name could not be enrolled among the people of God until the atonement money had been paid. The evident meaning of the type is, that it is not natural birth or training that gives a man his place among the people of God, but REDEMPTION, of which this atonement silver is a type. Like the Jews in the days of our Lord's life on earth who boasted, "We have Abraham to our father," while they were utterly destitute of Abraham's faith, so there are many now-a-days who make their boast in the religion of their forefathers, and garnish the tombs of the martyrs, while they reject the Son of God and deny the efficacy of His blood. But "it is the blood that maketh an atonement for the soul" (Lev. 17:11), and apart from that blood, and faith in Him who shed it, no name of any child of Adam can ever be written in "the Lamb's book of life." I beseech you to make no mistake on this point, dear friends. You are aware that all round there are men now preaching against the "blood of Christ" as that which brings the sinner nigh to God. They tell us that man is not a fallen being, but that there is some good principle in him, which, if it be properly nursed and cared for, will develop and make the man all right at last. Now this would be salvation apart from the blood of Christ, apart from *redemption* and *regeneration*. It is as if one was to say, " Your name will be enrolled among the people of God without any atonement money being paid." How utterly false is such a delusion ! How awful the doom of the propagators of such a soul-destroying lie ! Let us take heed and beware, lest the polluting stream come in contact with our spirits. Let God's people turn their backs straight upon all these emissaries of Satan, and not lend their ears to such preaching, even although it may be popular and the preachers themselves fill high places in the churches and universities.

The poor and the rich were to pay alike. At other times, when the people were bringing their free-will offerings to the Lord, each gave according to his ability— the rich more, the poor less, but in the matter of atonement all were alike. It is a sweeping and a humbling truth that " there is no difference " (Rom. 3:22), but it is the truth of God, and men must submit to it. The prince and the beggar, the drunkard and the Church member, must be saved exactly in the same way.

It is to this atonement silver that allusion is made in 1 Peter 1:18, 19— " Ye were not redeemed with corruptible things such as silver and gold, but with the *precious blood of Christ.* " And again, "The Church of God, which He hath purchased with His *own blood*" (Acts 20:28). REDEMPTION, by the blood of Christ, is the foundation on which the sinner rests. As the tenon (or hand) of the board took hold of the silver socket, so does the sinner's faith lay hold on Christ as his redemption. This is the rock on which he builds—" all other ground is sinking sand." Let all make sure work that they are resting wholly and solely on Christ, and not partly on the sockets and

partly on the sand of their own works. How easy it would
have been in the bustle to slip the tenon past the socket
and into the sand. Easier far for a sinner to miss Christ
and build on something else. But the testing day is coming
when the storm shall test every man's foundation—and,
O! what gaps may be made, even among those who were
supposed to be the people of God.

In the rearing up of the Tabernacle the sockets of
silver were the first part of the work. Before a board was
reared or a pin put in the Merarites laid down on the bare
sand of the desert the massive silver sockets. There
could have been no building apart from these. Corresponding with this, we find the Apostle Paul going into the
city of Corinth, when no vestige of a church was there,
and preaching " *Christ, and Him crucified* " (1 Cor. 2:2),
as the foundation for the sinner. We read that " many
believed " (Acts 18:8),   and he went on for " a year
and six months *teaching* the Word of God among them."
This was the founding of the " Church of God which is
at Corinth" (1 Cor. 1:2). The Apostle tells us in 1 Cor.
3:10, 11, that *Christ* was the foundation of their fellowship in the Church as He had been their salvation. The
names of Paul and Apollos were not linked with Christ
in the one or in the other, and this is the true foundation
of the fellowship of the Church. We are " called unto the
fellowship of His. Son Jesus Christ our Lord " (1 Cor.
1:9). Sectarian names must have no part in it, nor sectarian
doctrines either. These scatter and divide, but *His* name
and *His* Word gather into one and build up and bind
together. While we glory in His dear Name alone as the
foundation of our eternal salvation, let us hold it dear also
as the foundation of our fellowship one with another as
the Lord's redeemed.

Boards of Shittim Wood

(Exodus 26:15-25)

The framework of the Tabernacle consisted of boards of shittim wood. Twenty boards on the north side, twenty on the south, and eight along the western end. Each of the boards had two tenons by which it was connected with the two sockets of silver underneath.

Each of these boards represents a sinner saved by sovereign grace, who, having died as a child of Adam, has been raised from the dead, quickened into newness of life, and stands before God in Christ a member of the new creation. But let us see how all this was brought about. These boards were once in a different state. They were once stately acacia trees planted in the earth. The earth upheld them, its sap sustained them. Their roots were *in* and *of* the earth. But Jehovah had need of them for the building of His dwelling place, and the day came for the axe to be laid at their roots. They were cut down ; they died to the earth ; their connection with it was for ever severed. And such is the case with everyone in God's holy dwelling-place now being built upon the foundation Jesus Christ. They were once *in* and *of* the world, part of the old creation, men in the flesh. Their glory was like the " green bay tree," their life was of the world : they minded earthly things. But the sharp and mighty axe of truth, powerful in the Spirit's hand, fell upon the heart and conscience. It brought them low, confessing—" We all do fade as a *leaf* " ; our hope " hath He removed like a *tree* " (Isaiah 64:6 ; Job 19:10). Such is the first step in true conversion to God. There must be a " breaking down " before there can be a " raising up." This is the unequivocal testimony of the Scriptures, and in every case of conversion to God recorded therein we find the order is the same. Sinners were broken down before God.

They were made to bow and own their lost condition.
Pride was levelled and earthly glory brought to the dust.
The proud Pharisee on his way to Damascus was thrown
to the ground—literally, no doubt—but his boasted human
righteousness and pride were brought down as well. He
could say, " I have been crucified with Christ, and it is no
longer I that live" (Galatians 2:20). "I have suffered
the loss of all things, and do count them but dung "
(Phil. 3:8).   Here was a breaking down, a laying of the
axe at the root of the tree. See, again, the jailer at Philippi.
The earthquake shook the prison ; the power of God
awakened the jailer and made him cry out, " What must
I do to be saved ? " (Acts 16:30).   The three thousand
converted on the day of Pentecost were " pricked in their
hearts," and cried, " What shall we do ? "   (Acts 2:37).
Such is the way of God. This element is sadly lacking
now-a-days in much that professes to be the work of God.
There is extremely little of true breaking down ; indeed,
there is little of the kind of preaching that produces it.
Men in general are far too honey-mouthed and afraid to
offend their hearers, to tell out the honest truth of God.
There are few of the Jeremiah stamp of men, whose
ministry and appointed work is " to root out and to pull
down." Seldom were they more needed. Sinners are
hugged and cuddled into a sound but fatal sleep of self-
security. They know the Gospel in the letter, they profess
to believe it to be true, but there is no cutting off from the
world, no mark of Divine life in your souls. Let me put
this question straight to your souls—Have you ever been
brought low before God ? Have you ever bowed and
owned yourself a lost, ungodly sinner, fit only for the
burning ? Has your pride and earthly glory been brought
to the dust ? It matters little what you *know* or *do* if you
have not come down from your dignity ; you must be
brought down now, or in hell. What a downcoming yet

awaits the proud and haughty sinner. Down in the deep darkness of a lost eternity he will find all distinctions levelled, his companions demons, his associates the vile and refuse of earth. But we would not have anyone suppose that we deem it essential to true conversion that there must be what has been called a " striking down "— followed by a period of unconsciousness. No doubt, in times of special visitation, such things have occurred, and they not unfrequently have been made use of by the devil to turn people's eyes to such experiences and away from Christ. Lydia's heart was quietly opened at the river-side, no outward demonstration occurred. Hundreds have in like manner quietly passed from death to life. The point we insist on is this—no matter how or where it takes place—that the sinner *must go down before God.* He must allow the piercing edge of God's truth to penetrate his soul, laying him bare and bringing him down, before he can be raised up a converted man—a man in Christ.

The next point is, the tree was stripped of its boughs and cut down to the size prescribed by God.

It is after conversion that the "stripping process" begins in right earnest. As the truth of God is allowed to act on the believer's conscience he finds there are many superfluous things about him that require to be ".laid aside," things which in the days of his worldliness he considered to be right and proper, but they must now be " put off." They may not be " vile and refuse," but they are not of the *new creation* ; they are not consistent with his standing as a " citizen of Heaven " ; not in concord with his *pilgrim* character on earth. It requires no pressure to make him lay these aside. The sanctifying power of the Word effects the change as he submits his life and ways to the truth. The truth, in the power of the Spirit acting upon him, strips and fashions him according to the will of God. This is practical sanctification ; too practical to be adopted by mere professors of religion. Often have we seen such people turn suddenly round and walk no longer with us when the "stripping" and "squaring" process begins. The preaching of *grace* attracted them in crowds ; they extolled the preacher and the preaching, but immediately that the *truth* was brought to bear upon their life and walk and the claims of God told out from His Word they turned on the heel, like Pilate, asking— "What is truth ?" and made off as quickly as possible. The men of Nazareth would listen to the "*gracious* words" that proceeded from the Master's lips, but when He said, "I tell you of a *truth*," they threatened to cast Him over the brow of the hill　(Luke 4:22-29).　Thus it will be to the end wherever "grace and truth" are preached.

The boards were overlaid with gold. Their natural beauty was taken from them, and Divine beauty and glory given instead. Thus it is with the child of God. He may have no comeliness in the eyes of men, but the eyes of his God see him to be perfect in beauty, through the comeliness that *He* has put upon him　(Ezek. 16:14). He stands before God "accepted in the Beloved"— complete in Christ. Thus board after board was cut down and raised up, passing in type through death and resurrection to fill its place in the dwelling-place of God, and thus, in far more wondrous grace, are a people now being gathered out from the world—a people who have died and risen with Christ to be builded together into an habitation of God in the Spirit (Eph. 2:22).

The Bars

(Exodus 26:26-29)

The boards of shittim wood were framed together by bars of the same material overlaid with gold.

The truth here taught in type concerns the fellowship and unity of the people of God.

Each board stood erect on its own foundation. It had an individual standing of its own independent of all others. This shows the individual salvation and standing of the saints.

Each board was bound to the one beside it and to all the rest by bars of shittim wood. This shows the fellowship and unity of the saints.

The type reveals to us how Divine unity is formed and sustained and how it may be manifested.

We are not only units, nor do our privileges and responsibilities begin and end with ourselves. We have been bound up in the bundle of life with our fellow-saints, and the grace that made us members of the family of God had laid upon us the responsibility of being our brother's keeper. There is in the Scripture a vast, unique, and wide-spreading circle of truth presenting privileges and responsibilities to the saints of the present age concerning unity, which was unknown in ages past. We are verily guilty if we allow all this to lie unheeded, under the pretext that we are more deeply concerned about our individual life and walk than in seeking the salvation of the lost. These things have their ordered places, and ought to get the prominence due to them in the minds and activities of the saints, but surely not to the exclusion of the all weighty line of truth given by the same Lord to His people concerning their fellowship and responsibilities toward their fellow-saints and brethren. Of these it truly may be said, " These ought ye to have done, and not to leave the other undone " (Matt. 23:23).

The *bars* are *five* in number. They are first described generally, then particularly. Special attention is directed to the middle bar. We read in Exodus 26, verse 28, "And the middle bar *in the midst* of the boards shall rea :h from end to end," and in further explanation of this we read in Exodus 36:33—"And He made the middle bar *to shoot through the boards* from one end to the other." The middle bar would thus bind all the boards together. The many boards by it were framed into one tabernacle, and thus formed a manifest visible unity. An onlooker could see the outward unity of the board but not the bar that formed and sustained it. It was hid within the heart of the boards where no rude hand of man could break or displace it. And thus it is with that which binds together and unites the saints of God. The saints of God are one— one with Christ and one with each other. No power on earth or in hell can pluck the feeblest lamb from the Shepherd's bosom or wrench the feeblest member from the body of Christ. The deep mysterious oneness that exists between the Risen Head and His members is Divine and eternal. So is the union of the members one with another. The Church, viewed as the body of Christ, embraces every child of God throughout the world. It *includes* all who have life in Christ, and *excludes* all who are dead in sin.

But there is another aspect of the Church presented in the Scriptures : that is, as gathered together unto Christ on earth, as God's witness in a dark and evil world. It is concerning the Church in this aspect that the type before us speaks. We see here how a company of the people of God are divinely gathered and fitly framed together. Such was the Church which was at Jerusalem (Acts 8:1),   the Church of God which was at Corinth (1 Cor. 1:2), and the Churches of Galatia (Gal. 1:2). They were composed of believers only, and they were gathered unto God's center and united in God's way. They are the Divine pattern of Churches of God. As the bar in " *the midst* " of the boards united them all, so does the Lord " *in the midst* " unite His gathered saints. Once in

cold contempt and scorn they crucified Him with robbers,
" on either side one, and *Jesus in the midst* " (John 19:
18). On that center cross every eye was fixed. The Holy
Sufferer there was *the* object of derision, and upon Him
alone the mob did vent their hatred and their scorn.
By and by, when the ransomed throng, completed and
glorified, shall gather around the throne, the " Lamb in
the *midst* " shall be the object of their worship and the
theme of their song. " Jesus in the midst " of that bright
glory shall be their center, and His dear, uniting Name
alone shall beam on every brow. Other names and other
bonds of union shall have no place there. Down below on
the earth, the " outcasts of Israel " and the " dispersed
of Judah," so long scattered and peeled, will be gathered
in blessed union, their envies and their jealousies gone,
united by the same endearing Name, for " Unto *Him* shall
the gathering of the people be " (Gen. 49:10).   During
the present age of His rejection by the world, the promise
is yea and amen to us, that " where two or three are gathered
together in *My Name*, there am I *in the midst* " (Matt.
18:20). This is the center and the rallying point for
the saints of God, and where His Name and His Person
alone are sought unto there will be unity blessed and
Divine. It was so in the beginning. Sects and parties
bearing different names had no place in the early Church.

> " The Saints were of one heart and soul,
> And love Divine inspired the whole."

By and by, men began to force their pet doctrines into
undue prominence, and from among their " own-selves
did men arise, speaking perverse things to draw away the
disciples after them" (Acts 20:30). The factions
thus created by these doctrines soon began to assume more
definite form, and other *names* came to the front alongside
the name of Jesus. " One saith, I am of Paul ; and

another, I of Apollos" (1 Cor. 1:12). Sectarianism,
created and fostered within the hearts of the saints,
appeared in outward form. Sects and parties sprang
bearing the names of their founders, or of their peculiar
doctrines, and thus the leaven wrought until, after centuries
of divisions, secessions, and disruptions, the professing
Church of Christ presents to an infidel and the scoffing
world, the divided, Babel-like front of several hundreds
of sects, each clamouring for the mastery and the credit
of being the *true* Church. Some of these are grossly
unclean and their doctrine entirely destitute of truth.
Some are more evangelical in doctrine, but miserably
corrupt in practice ; while others are largely composed
of those who neither have themselves been converted, nor
believe that any one else can be sure of being saved. The
unhappy saints who are mixed up in this mass of confusion
and iniquity, groaning over the sad state of affairs, are
glad to escape from their trammels at times, to get a handful of the corn of Heaven where-ever they can find it. Hid
among the wreckage, few of the saints know each other,
and they who are to dwell together in the Father's house
for ever, are all but strangers to each other here. Efforts
have been often made to bring about a change, and draw
the saints together. Prayer Unions, Evangelistic Unions,
and Young Men's Associations have been formed. Con-
ferences and tea-meetings have been held, and many other
schemes devised to draw together and unite the scattered
sheep of the blood bought flock of God. It has been found
to be profitable and refreshing thus to meet, discarding
all sectarian names and ecclesiastical titles, simply as
disciples of the one and only Lord. The saints have
strengthened one another's hands, and sought to encourage
one another's hearts in God, like David and Jonathan in.
the wood ; but, strange to say, many have parted to return
to their favorite sects again, and to support the creeds

and associations that keep them divided from each
other. The roots of sectarianism are left unjudged, and its
trammels bind them still. The saints who meet around
a common tea-table to enjoy the fellowship of one another
refuse to gather around the table of the Lord together.
If it be so passing sweet to meet around the one dear
Name on a week-day or at a conference, why should they
not continually do so ? The one uniting Name and Person
is surely the same yesterday, to-day, and for ever, and
would gather and bind them together continually on earth
as He will in Heaven. If the saints of God would judge the
sin of sectarianism in their hearts and purge themselves
out from the mixed multitude gathering unto Jesus Christ
the Lord, they would surely prove the power and blessed-
ness of the word, " Behold, how good and how pleasant it is
for brethren to dwell together in unity " (Psalm 133:1),
and under the shepherd rule of the Lord Jesus they would
be made once more as one flock to lie down in green
pastures by the waters of quietness.

The boards were bound together *outwardly* by four
bars of shittim wood passed through rings of gold. In early
days, when " all who believed were together," when the
saints were of one heart and soul, and when around the
unseen but *real* presence they were gathered, we read that
" they continued steadfastly in the Apostles' doctrine and
fellowship, and in breaking of bread and in prayers "
(Acts 2:42). These were the outward bars that bound
them together and pressed them to the center. The
" Apostles' doctrine "—as it is to be found in the Word
—the faith once delivered to the saints in its entirety and
purity must be held fast and submitted to, if a church
is to be preserved in unity ; perfectly joined together of
one accord and of one mind. No part brought into undue
prominence ; no part suppressed. This is where the germ
of division has its rise, and where associations and unions

fail. An association formed on the principle that certain truths must not be mentioned is an association of sects. It is not united by the "Apostles' doctrine," and cannot be of God. The doctrine forms the "fellowship," "the breaking of bread" expresses it, and "the prayers" lay hold on God for power to sustain it. The *ring* is the emblem of *love*. The truth must be held and used in love, not in pride or bigotry. "This is the love of God, that we keep His Commandments" (1 John 5:3), and "By this shall all men know that ye are My disciples if ye have *love* one to another" (John 13:35).

Coverings and the Curtains
(Exodus 26:1-14)

There were two sets of coverings and two sets of curtains. The coverings consisted of an outer covering of badgers' skins and an inner covering of rams' skins dyed red. The outer set of curtains was of goats' hair, and the inner set of fine linen, with blue, purple and scarlet. The outer set of curtains is properly named "the tent," and the inner set "the Tabernacle."

We will consider them in their typical character as pointing onward to Christ, in whom the Father dwelt, also to the Church of God corporately, and the saints individually, in whom He now dwells and walks.

I. THE COVERING OF BADGERS' SKINS.—This was the outermost and visible covering. It was to protect from the sun's scorching rays and from the storms of the desert. It had no form or comeliness, and there was no outward beauty to attract the gaze of men. The Tabernacle was all glorious within, with boards overlaid with gold and curtains of needle-work, but these were only seen by God's anointed priest who stood within the Holy Place. The badgers' skin is mentioned once again in Scripture, and there as used for sandals to separate from and to protect

the feet of God's redeemed on the burning sands of the
desert (Ezekiel 16:10). The badgers' skin is therefore
connected with the separation and earthly pilgrim character
of the people of God. It gives them protection from that
which would hurt them in such a character. The type had
its full answer in the Lord Jesus while He lived on earth.

Fairest of the fair, " Chiefest among ten thousand," to
those who knew Him, yet despised and rejected of men,
the marred visage of the Man of Sorrows presented no
attraction to the eye of the world. They saw a lonely Man
without an earthly home. They saw Him weep and heard
Him sigh, but they desired Him not, nor cared to ask
from whence He came. Enough for them to know He was
" the carpenter," the son of Mary, the Nazarene. With
mocking scorn and ribald jest they hurried the Man of
Sorrows to the cross. Oh that our souls may earnestly gaze
upon that sight ! The thorn-crowned brow, the cruel,
heartless mob, the foul and base reproach they heaped
upon the dear and holy Sufferer. Such was the world
then, such was the treatment of the Son of God, and such
is the world still and ever will be. As our souls gaze upon
that blessed Face we shall grow like Him ; as we grow
like Him we shall suffer shame and reproach for His Name.
How little of this reproach is known by the saints of God.
Many are reigning now where He was cast out, and caressed
where He was scorned. Is it so with you, beloved ? Have
you gained the world's approving smile ? Is your name in
fame and esteem among His foes ? Surely, if it be so, you
must be very unlike your Lord. But the offence of the
cross and the reproach of Christ yet remain to all who
follow the despised and rejected Nazarene. Suffering and
shame will attend their steps. Tears and sobs will often
mark their path. The reigning time will come, and for
that let us patiently wait. The Nazarene shall yet be
seated on His throne, the pierced hand shall hold the

sceptre of universal power, and on the brow, once rudely wreathed with thorns, shall rest the many crowns. The badgers' skin covering shall then be rolled off, and a glorious Church shall be presented to her heavenly Bridegroom.

" Thou too shalt reign, He will not wear His crown of joy alone, And earth, His royal Bride shall see, beside Him on His Throne."

II. THE COVERING OF RAMS' SKINS DYED RED.—This is the type of consecration unto death. The ram was used for sacrifice, notably so in the consecration of the priesthood (Lev. 8). As the *lamb* typifies the meek and lowly Jesus submissive unto death, so the *ram* speaks of the vigour and strength of the Lord, and of that fixed purpose of heart which led Him on in the path of unreserved devotedness to God even unto death. The ram's skin put upon the Tabernacle reminds us of the setting apart of the Church unto God ; as the blood put upon the ear, the hand, and the foot of the priest reminds us of our members being redeemed and cleansed by Him. Consecration is a very real and intensely practical thing. It is not an outward action, but a deep-seated fixed purpose of heart. It includes a great deal more than is attached to the term by those who speak of " entire consecration." It is very easy for the lips to sing—

> " My all is on the altar ; " and
> " Take my life and let it be ;
>   Consecrated Lord to Thee."

but are we in truth prepared for this ? We learn the meaning of " entire consecration " by the side of the cross. That holy, devoted One who " set His face steadfastly " to the place of death, " despising the shame," is the example and measure of " entire consecration."

> " Unmoved by Satan's subtile wiles,
>   By suffering, shame and loss ;
> His path, uncheered by earthly smiles,
>   Led only to the Cross."

We are called to follow in His steps and to yield ourselves to God. An Apostle once could say, " I am ready
to die for the Name of the Lord Jesus," and he suffered
the loss of all for Christ. This is an easy-going age. Grace
is preached, but its demands are little heard of. The
claims of Christ as Lord are deemed to be " non-essential,"
and true devotedness is branded a legality. Blessed it is
to know that our Lord can duly estimate, and will one day
own that true consecration which brought upon His
loved ones here the merciless judgment of their carnal
brethren and the slander and scorn of the world. His
hand shall yet roll off the badgers' skin that covers it now,
and for this let us patiently wait.

III. THE CURTAINS OF GOATS' HAIR.—They were the
memorials of atonement made. The daily sin-offering was
a kid of the goats (Numbers 28:15) ; and for the cleansing
from sin—the goat was the chosen victim   (see Lev. 16).
The double curtain hung above the door may indicate
that the only ground of approach to God was by sin being
put away, and that the memorial thereof was continually
before the eye of the priest as he entered the sanctuary of
God. The curtains were coupled together by loops of
goats' hair and taches of copper. This reminds us that the
only unity approved of God must be in righteousness and
holiness. There must be no conniving at holiness or
trifling with sin.

IV. THE CURTAINS OF FINE LINEN.—They were only
visible to the priest within the Holy Place. They represent
the glories of Christ in resurrection and of His saints as
risen with Him. The *fine linen* speaks of purity and
righteousness. The *blue* is Heaven's own color, and tells
of the heavenly character of the Son of God. The *scarlet*
is the color of earth, and reminds us of His earthly glory
as Son of Man. The *purple* is the combination of blue
and scarlet, and points on to that time when the glory of

the heavenly and the glory of the earthly shall have their
center and manifestation in His blessed Person. The
cherubim tell His majesty and power. The curtains were
coupled and "joined" together by loops of blue and
taches of gold, and thus the several curtains were made
to form "one Tabernacle." The saints as risen with
Christ are all united now and "perfectly joined together"
in Divine and heavenly union. The full display and manifestation of this will be seen in glory, but faith even now
discerns it while in communion with God within His holy
temple, and seeks to own and rest upon it in subjection
to His Word amid the discord and division of the present
time, "Endeavouring to keep the unity of the Spirit in
the bond of peace " (Eph. 4:3).

THE HOLY PLACE

The Tabernacle, or Tent, was divided into two distinct apartments, differing in size and name. The first and largest of these is called the Holy Place, the second, the " Holy of Holies," or " Holiest of All."

The Holy Place contained the altar of incense, the table of shew-bread, and the golden candlestick. It was the place of priestly privilege and service, and within its precincts the sons of Aaron the priest accomplished daily " the service of God " (Heb. 9:6). No foot of man was allowed to tread, or hand of man to serve within its sacred walls, save that of a consecrated priest.

The congregation of Israel had access to the outer court but no further. They might bring their offerings to the brazen altar, but to the golden altar within the Holy Place they were forbidden to come.

The typical teaching here points on to the place of vast and unique blessing pertaining to believers of the present age as " priests to God," a title of inexpressible blessing, little understood or appreciated by many of those to whom through grace it belongs.

For the sake of those who are young in Christ and newly come to the faith, it may be profitable here to meditate on it a little.

In Israel, the priesthood was vested in a single family —the family of Aaron, of the tribe of Levi. Natural birth into that family was the only way of sharing its privileges.

The title was hereditary, and passed on to the descendants. In the present age of grace and spiritual blessing it is exactly the opposite. By natural birth all are shut out from God, and by spiritual birth, or being "born again," all are made priests. Such is one of the marked distinctions between the ages of law and grace, and one of the broad outlines which mark Christianity as entirely differing from Judaism. In the family of God, born from above, there are no such distinctions recognized as "priests" and "common people." The words so filled with grace and blessing—" Ye are a chosen generation, a royal *priesthood*, an holy nation, a peculiar people " (1 Peter 2:9)— are applicable to all the saints of God. The weakest and feeblest of the redeemed of the Lord may adopt them and enjoy the privileges pertaining to them with the most mature in grace. Attainments and gifts come not in here. They have their severally ordered places, but the priesthood, with the whole range and sphere of blessing and privilege attaching to it, is the birthright of all the saints.

Beloved, do we esteem the exceeding riches of this grace of God ? Or are we enslaved by a false humility to take a lower place and to stand afar off in a haze of bondage and fear? The precious blood has made us near, the Spirit of sonship dwells within, and it is the joy of the Father's heart to see the face and hear the voice of all His children. In condescending grace He stooped to lift us from the depths of our ruin, and, not satisfied with merely rescuing us, He raised us to the rank of " an holy priesthood to offer up spiritual sacrifices acceptable to God by Jesus Christ" (1 Peter 2:5) within His holy Temple. The heaven in which we are to sing for ever is open now to faith ; the great High Priest has gone within, carrying with Him our title, and He tells us to draw near, and by Him to " offer the sacrifice of praise to God continually, that is, the fruit of our lips giving thanks to His Name " (Heb. 13:15).

The Holy Places made with hands are the figures of the true heavens. The priest of Israel, accepted through

the sacrifices offered at the altar, made clean by the water
of the laver, and anointed with the holy oil, is the type of a
believer accepted in the Beloved, cleansed by the washing
of regeneration and by the Word of God, anointed with
the Holy Ghost, and thereby fitted to draw nigh to God.
The blood of Jesus is the title, the daily cleansing by the
Word is the condition, and the Spirit of God the power
for fulfilling the functions of our priestly calling (see
Heb. 10:19-22 ; Eph. 2:18).

The *door* of the tent was an hanging of blue, purple
and scarlet, on five pillars of shittim wood, overlaid and
crowned with *gold*, and set in sockets of *copper*. This was
the entrance to the Holy Place. It was of the same super-
ficial measurement as the gate of the Court, but it was
double the height and only half the width. The difference
is significant. The gate of the Court was *wide*, the door
of the sanctuary was *narrow*. The *gate* was for all, the
door was only for the priests.

There is a fulness and a narrowness in the things of
God which we do well to mark. The Gospel of the grace
of God is for the *world*, and the gate is wide enough for all.
The privileges and blessings of the House of God are only
for the saints, and the *door* is therefore narrow. Let us
remember this. It is an inversion of God's order, to restrict
the Gospel to a few, and to admit the world to fill the
children's place. There ought to be a distinctive line
drawn in preaching the Word between the children of
God and the unconverted, and a right dividing of the word
of truth, giving to each his portion. This has been fear-
fully set aside in Christendom. Mixed congregations of
saints and sinners are frequently addressed and prayed for
as " beloved brethren," and the " children's bread " is
dealt out to all and several alike. The ungodly are made
to believe that they are " inheritors of the Kingdom of
God," and are thus hardened in their guilt and condemned

in their hypocrisy. The door of the Church is thrown wide
open to the unconverted, and the table of the Lord and His
worship is defiled and degraded by the world being
admitted to them. The Lord does not hold any guiltless
who do, or who countenance and uphold such unhallowed
deeds. With Holy jealousy for His Name, He has put a
fence of truth around the "holy things," and if men with
impious hand throw it down or teach their fellows to
disregard it He will yet avenge Himself upon them. May
the Lord awaken the consciences of His saints to see the
deep dishonor done unto His Name, and the eternal
ruin brought upon the souls of men, by allowing and
instructing unconverted men to presumptuously take part
in the worship of God. The case of King Uzziah, who in
the pride of his heart once entered the door of the Holy
Place with a censer in his hand to burn incense and was
smitten with leprosy, may well be a warning to such
(2 Chron. 26:16-19) ; and also that of Korah and his
company, who were destroyed by the judgment of God
for assuming to be priests when they were not (see Num.
16).

Within the Holy Place the altar of incense, the golden
candlestick, and the table of shew-bread stood. The
service of the priest consisted in burning incense at the
altar, in trimming the lamps of the candlestick, and in
eating bread at the table. These are figures of the service
of the heavenly priesthood, which we will consider more
fully in connection with the respective vessels. May it
be our happy daily experience, beloved, to consciously
abide in his Tabernacle under the shadow of the wings
of the Almighty. Hid in His secret presence, in the Lord's
own pavilion, our souls shall be safe from the arrows of the
wicked and the strife of tongues, and, having found the
abiding title to enter there in the blood of the Lamb of
God, may we be preserved in a condition of cleanness by

the continuous application of the Word to our thoughts and words and ways. Thus, walking in the ungrieved power of the Holy Ghost with ardent longing of soul, shall we be saying—" One thing have I desired of the Lord, *that will I seek after* : that I may dwell in the House of the Lord all the days of my life, to behold the beauty of the Lord, and to enquire in His temple " (Psa. 27:4).

Altar of Incense
(Exodus 30:1-10)

The Altar of incense stood within the Holy Place. It was made of shittim wood and gold, and had a crown of gold around its top.

Here let us distinguish clearly between this vessel and the altar of burnt-offering.

The altar before the door was made of shittim wood and copper ; the altar within the Holy Place of shittim wood and gold. The copper altar was the place of sacrifice ; the golden altar was the place of incense. There was continual bloodshed at the one ; perpetual incense at the other.

The glories of Christ appear in both altars. Christ on the cross in the altar of burnt-offering ; Christ risen and glorified in the altar of incense. Down here He stood *for us* in the place of death and judgment, and met our deep need as *sinners*. Up there He lives *for us* still in the presence of God, meeting all our need as His *saints* and *worshippers*. By His sacrifice we were redeemed, forgiven, accepted, and brought nigh to God ; by His intercession we are maintained in communion. It is Christ to begin with, Christ to go on with, and Christ for evermore.

Let us draw near and gaze upon this golden altar with its crown.

" Rise, my soul, behold, 'tis Jesus ;
Jesus fills thy wondering eyes."

It was made of *shittim wood* and *gold*. Shittim wood, the type of His perfect humanity ; gold, of His Divine glory as the Son of God. There was no gold outside. When Jesus was down here He was as really the God-man as He is now within the heavens, but the gold was hid from the eyes of men. He passed through earth in humiliation, not in glory. Although He was then, as now, " the Mighty God," He appeared among men in the " form of a servant " and in " fashion as a man." But up there where He now is the *glorified* One, the gold is seen in all its rightness, and there is no veil to hide it. But He is as really *the Man* Christ Jesus now as when He stood with the little child in his arms and pressed it to his bosom. He is as truly the Sympathizer now as when He stood at Lazarus' tomb and wept ; and He would have us to know and enjoy Him thus. He is as truly engaged for us now in the midst of all His glory as He was when, amid His woe, He loved us unto blood. His love can never grow cold, for it is like Himself : " the same yesterday, and to-day, and for ever." O what comfort to the soul to know Him there as " the golden altar before the throne " (Rev. 8:3), the Ever-living One who maketh intercession for His downcast, weary people (Heb. 7:25 ; Rom. 8: 34). Look up to Heaven, ye crushed and burdened saints, and see the Mighty God engaged to bring you through. The sharpest pang you feel affects His heart ; the deepest woe you bear is familiar to Him who was the Man of Sorrows. He trod the same path Himself, and met with all the forms of suffering that it is possible for His saints to meet, and thus His sympathy is the sympathy of the perfect Man, and His power the power of the Mighty God. He can be " touched with a feeling of our infirmities," because He is Man ; He is " able to succour " the tried and tempted, because He is God.

It had a crown of gold. " We see Jesus crowned with

glory and honour" (Heb. 2:9). There was no crown around the altar outside the door : nothing but blood and ashes there. This reminds us of Calvary. There was no diadem of glory on the brow of the Holy Sufferer there ; only the tangled thorn-crown with the ruby blood-drops —jewels of priceless value to the believer's heart. But on that very brow, where wicked hands entwined a crown of

The Altar of Incense

thorns, the hand of God has put a crown of glory and honor. His "sufferings" are past, His "glories" must follow. The saints of God already own His dominion and yield Him obedience ; and, by and by, when He comes to claim the Kingdom and to put down the false one, the Anti-Christ who shall rule earth's kings, the "many crowns" shall all be *His*, and every kindred and people and tongue shall then join to sing—

> " Bring forth the royal diadem "
> And crown Him Lord of all.

It is mockery, in this age of His rejection, to invite " all people that on earth do dwell" to "sing to the Lord with cheerful voice," when the bulk of them are the children of the devil, and the enemies of God. The world disowns His name and spurns His authority. Those whom He has won for Himself out of Satan's dominion, and made unto Himself "a kingdom and priests unto God and His Father" (Rev. 1:6), these, and only these, can truly worship God with cheerful voice.

"*And Aaron shall burn thereon sweet incense every morning*" (Exod. 30:7). "*By Him* let us offer the sacrifice of praise to God continually" (Heb. 13:15). "*Every day* will I bless Thee, and I will *praise* Thy name for ever and ever" (Psa. 145:2). "Blessed are they that dwell in Thy house : they will be still *praising* Thee" (Psa. 84:4).

Christ is the altar, believers are priests, and Heaven is the place of worship. God's earthly place of worship was first the Tabernacle, then the Temple, but since the Cross of Christ there has been no earthly place of worship. Our golden altar is in Heaven, and there by faith we pass in spirit, and worship God by Him. The body may be on a lonely couch, or in a prison, as Paul and Silas were in Macedonia, in the inner prison.

> "But prison bars cannot control
> The flight, the freedom of the soul."

Their spirits were around the golden altar within the heavenly temple, and "at midnight they prayed and sang praises to God." Not only on the first day of the week, when, with disciples, we congregate around the Person of Immanuel, but at all times in all places it is the believer's privilege to be in a worshipping condition of soul. "My praise shall be *continually* of Thee" (Psa. 71:6). "Giving thanks *always* for all things" (Eph. 5:20).

Brethren beloved, is this our daily employment ? Is this the atmosphere we breathe by road, and rail and at our daily work ? If it were so, we should see no discontented grumbling saints, no captious, quarrelling brethren. Ah, no ! When brethren fall out by the way, it is because some of them have left the "spot where spirits blend," and once away from the warmth of His love, saints can do anything.

In the beginning of the Gospel of Luke we see Zacharias, the Jewish priest, by the side of the incense altar in the earthly temple, and the people *without* praying ; but in the closing verses of that Gospel, the saints are gathered to worship *Him* whom they had seen carried up to Heaven. Earthly priests and vestments, earthly altars and temples, are suited to the world. It must have a religion suited to its senses : requiring no spiritual life or Holy Ghost energy ; but why the living heavenly saints should seek the living Christ among these dead forms we do not know.

THE INCENSE. It was an holy perfume, composed of four spices, prepared according to the command of Jehovah. None was to be made like unto it, upon penalty of being cut off from the people of Jehovah. Solemn words for a day like ours, when license under the name of liberty desecrates the most sacred things of God. The incense is the type of that holy fragrance which did, and ever will, ascend from the ways and character of the Lord Jesus unto the Father.

When we bring our praises unto God, let them be *of* Him, His Person, His character, His worth. These are the spices like unto which none are to be made. No worshipping of saints, dead or living ; no prayers or praises to the Virgin or Apostles, or about ourselves or our own attainments. " Worthy is the Lamb " is Heaven's song : let it be ours. What a sham is all the instrumental music used in what is called the worship of God. How abominable to Him is the song of the most talented orchestra of unconverted sinners. A handful of His blood-bought saints gathered in some lonely corner telling out the worth of Jesus into the Father's open ear from burning hearts, is incense of a sweet savour unto Him. To such—

" God graciously is bending
To hear each feeble groan."

The fire was to be taken from the altar of sacrifice.
No strange incense, no strange fire was allowed. The fire
which had fed on the victim was to burn on the altar of
incense, and the blood of the sacrifice was to stain it horns.
Thus in our worship are we ever to have Calvary in view.
" A Lamb as it had been slain " in the midst of the throne
will keep Calvary for ever before the glorified saints. We
can only worship God as we live beside the Cross. Nadab
and Abihu offered strange fire and died before the Lord
(Lev. 10:1). They were true priests. They had true
incense ; but they used strange fire, not the fire of the
altar which came from Heaven (Lev. 9:24). The only
power for worship is the Holy Ghost : all else is strange
fire. The oft repeated " Hallelujah," the frequent bursts
of "Praise the Lord," the words so oft repeated by
thousands every Sunday, " Glory be to the Father and to
the Son," if they are not the fruit of the Spirit's operation
within the soul, they are only " great swelling words of
vanity."

Sentimental religion is common. Unholy familiarity
in the things of God and a corresponding irreverent way
of addressing Him are rapidly increasing. " Dear Jesus "
—" Precious Jesus "—are expressions often flippantly
uttered by professing Christians. But when Stephen, filled
with the Holy Ghost, gazed steadfastly on the blessed
One, he said, " *Lord* Jesus, receive my spirit " ; and on
the Damascus road, when Saul of Tarsus saw His glory
and heard His voice, he said, " *Lord*, what wilt thou have
me to do ? "

May our souls be kept in His fear, giving Him reverence, hid in his pavilion, worshipping in His presence.
Soon we shall bow in ransomed bodies in the presence

of the throne of God and the Lamb, to praise Him ever-more.

The Table of Shewbread

Table of Shewbread
(Exodus 25:23-30)

The next vessel of the Holy Place is the Table of Shrewbread with its twelve loaves.

It was made of shittim wood and overlaid with gold, with a golden crown around the top. There was a border of an handbreadth, then a second crown of gold around it. Twelve loaves made of fine flour and overlaid with frankincense lay upon the table within the inner crown in two rows. At the close of every week they were removed by the priest and replaced by twelve fresh loaves, the priesthood receiving the former as their food. The table stood within the Holy Place on the north side, over against the candlestick of gold.

Let us seek in the fear of God to gather the precious truth the Spirit brings before our souls in this expressive type. The table with its bread presents a double aspect of the truth : it has a Godward and a manward side. First, it stood before the Lord, upholding and presenting as unto Him the holy bread ; and next, it was the place at which the priesthood served and found their food. The table itself represents the Risen Christ—Christ as the God-man glorified in the heavens, appearing now in the presence of God. But not only was there a table, there was also bread—a loaf for every tribe in Israel's camp. The twelve tribes were represented there in all their perfectness and unity, the small as well as the great. The royal Judah, the priestly Levi, and little Benjamin, had each their representative loaf there all covered with the pure and fragrant frankincense. When the eye of Jehovah rested on that Holy table it rested on His people too. Not one of them was forgotten there, for the bread was to be " continually " before the Lord. The word translated " shrewbread " means " the presence bread " or " bread of the faces " (see the margin). It was ever in Jehovah's presence, and continually before His face. His holy eye was ever looking down upon it, feasting, as it were, upon it with satisfaction.

And, O beloved friends, with what unbounded joy does the Father's eye now look upon that glorified Man within the heavens ? Can human heart conceive, or angel tongue express, with what ineffable delight His eye at this moment rests upon His glorified Son ? We cannot gauge the measure of the love wherewith the Father loves the Son ; but, whatever the measure of that love may be, we are sharers in it. We are loved, and blessed, and " accepted in the Beloved." The entire company of the saints are complete in Him. They are continually before the Father's face, presented and covered over with the fragrant frankincense of His peerless Name and perfect work, and it is their birthright to sing, with heart and soul and voice—

" So dear, so very dear to God, more dear I cannot be ;
   The love wherewith He loves the Son, *such* is His love to me.'

The golden crown around the shrewbread kept it in it place, and protected it from falling off as the table was borne on the Levites' shoulders along the desert. Not only does Christ bring us into this place of nearness and blessing, but He keeps us there. No doubt our stumbling steps down here would very soon have caused us to forfeit it all, had not He undertaken to keep it for us and us for it.

But the golden crown encircled all the loaves clasping them, as it were, on the table. And we are encircled by love Eternal, Omnipotent, and Divine ; love that had no beginning and shall never have an end.

But there is another aspect of the table and the bread, upon which it will be profitable for us to meditate a little.

Jehovah provided this table for His priests, and the " presence bread " became their food. They fed upon that holy bread before the Lord, thus sharing, as it were, His own delight in it and His own appreciation of it. And we are called to share His joy in Christ and to feed upon the Bread of God. We have been called unto the fellowship of the Father and of the Son, and it is our privilege to enjoy that fellowship from day to day. Communion with God is what we have here expressed in type. The priest was called to be a partaker with His God, and this is communion. There was worship at the altar and communion at the table. At the altar, the priest was a giver, but at the table he was a *giver* and a *receiver*. Every Sabbath, he came with fresh shewbread to present before Jehovah, and every Sabbath he received, as if from Jehovah's hand, His bread to eat. The former expresses our presentation of Christ to God when we draw near to worship, the latter shows His presentation of Christ to us, as the Bread upon which our souls may feed.

The priesthood had their portion in the offerings of the Lord, and upon these they might feed individually, and at other times and places. But the priesthood feeding upon the shewbread at the table within the Holy Place, would seem to point to that special expression of communion with God and with each other which believers now enjoy, when gathered around the Lord's table on the Lord's-day to eat the Lord's Supper. The same love that provided a table in the midst of that howling desert, and gathered His priests around it to eat, has spread for us a table too, ànd called us to it, like Mephibosheth of old, to "eat bread as one of the king's sons."

" *Thou* preparest a table before me in the presence of mine enemies." The table is not ours, but *His*. He provided it, He furnishes and orders it, and we are only His guests. With what jealous care He guards His table we may surely learn, from the words He uses in describing it. It was a " pure " table ; the bread upon it was " holy ", it stood within the " Holy Place " ; and those who surrounded it were a " holy priesthood," anointed with the " holy oil " and clad in " holy garments." Surely " holiness becometh Thine house, O Lord, for ever " ; and " God is greatly to be feared in the assembly of the saints, and to be had in reverence of all them that are about Him " (Psalm 93:5 ; 89:7).

It has ever been the work of the enemy to seek to corrupt and degrade the holy things, and the very strength of his attack seems to have concentrated itself in all ages upon the Lord's table and the Lord's Supper. Highest of all the Church's privileges down here, it has ever been Satan's aim to deprive her of it. And to what extent he has succeeded, a careful comparison of what passes for " the Lord's Supper " with what is written concerning it the Word will suffice to show. Hardly a remaining trace of that holy, simple feast, as it was instituted by the Lord, and first celebrated by His disciples in the upper room, can now be seen among the sects of Christendom. The " Mass " of Popery and the " Sacrament " of Protestantism are alike a caricature of the simple feast. By their forms and ceremonies they have virtually set the *Lord's* Supper aside, and denied the Lord the right of governing His table. But the pattern is still in the Book, for all who are willing to follow it.

In connection with those who were invited to this shewbread table, there are two or three points I wish you to notice. We are first told who were *not* to come, then, who *were* to come, and next, *how often* they were to come. You see the Lord was very particular in telling them all about it. There was nothing left for them to fill in or arrange. First, then, who were *not* to eat ? " There shall no *stranger* eat of the holy thing : a *sojourner* of the priest or an *hired servant* shall not eat of the holy thing " (Lev. 22:10).

Here are three classes who were prohibited from partaking of the priesthood's food. They represent three classes of unconverted people. " No stranger." This is one of the descriptions given of man in his natural state (see Eph. 2:11). " No sojourner of the priest." Perhaps an intimate friend come to stay with him for a time, but when the Sabbath day came round he *must* be told that he cannot enter the Holy Place or eat the holy things. Human nature would recoil from this. What more natural than to take his friend with him ! Perhaps it might do him good, and teach him to revere the God of Israel ! But human reasonings are invariably opposed to Scripture, and, when allowed to supplant it, apostasy is the result. And this is done to a fearful extent in the present day. The children of believing parents when they come of age, and their friends and relatives when they come to visit, are often brought forward to the Lord's table in a slip-shod way, without much question whether they are " born again " or not. It is much easier for the flesh to bring them there, than to honestly tell them that they must take

their place among those who are "without" until it be
manifest to all that they are truly converted. Dear friends,
are you all clear before God as to this matter ? Take
care that you do not, under the plea of a false charity,
bring the Moabite into the congregation of the Lord. It
is easy to make oneself believe that either child or relative
is converted, especially if our discernment be small, and
if our minds be set on having them in among the saints.
It is better in all such cases to leave it to the discernment
of others. Do not allow the honey of human nature to
hinder faithful dealing and careful examination, of those
who seek a place at the table of the Lord.

"An *hired servant* shall not eat thereof." A man
working for salvation is not to be there, yet many do go,
because they are told it is "a means of grace," and that
in the Sacrament "Christ communicateth to us the
benefits of redemption." Such is the lawlessness of man,
leading to a complete subversion of the order of God.
But there were others also to be excluded.

"What man soever of the *seed of Aaron* is a *leper*, or
hath a *running issue*, he shall not eat of the holy things
until he be clean " (Lev. 22:4).

It was no question here of his being a priest. That
point was settled, yet by reason of *defilement* he was for
the present disqualified from enjoying the privileges of
the priesthood. Now, this is a very solemn thing. A true
believer may become tainted with the leprosy of indulged
and cherished evil either doctrinal or moral, so that he
becomes unfit to hold communion with a holy God, or
to be in the fellowship of the saints. Such was the case
with some at Corinth. One had gone on indulging and
practicing sin, until it became necessary to excommunicate
him, and the saints were told to put him away. Sin is
contagious, and if one defiled is permitted to go in and
out as he did before, the disease will rapidly spread. It is

not a question of his ceasing to be a Christian, for he
may be restored to God and to His people. But for the
present he is unclean, and must be treated as such. How
all this is denied and set aside by those who urge that
because the table is the Lord's, therefore *all* His people
may come to it! A strange deduction from such solemn
premises! Surely a more worthy deduction would be,
that " seeing the table is the Lord's, therefore *He* must
rule it, and His will is to be done, and His authority
owned, by those who assemble around it."

There is yet another extreme which, in seeking to act
out the will of the Lord, we need to guard against, and that
is to exclude any one whom God has bidden come. Here
comes a *lame* priest, and yet another *blind*. Now, what
is to be done with them? One does not see clearly,
another cannot walk aright or keep rank with those who
do. It would be very natural for us to say that for such
defects they ought not to share the fellowship of their
brethren; but Jehovah says, " he *shall* eat the bread of
his God, both of the most holy and of the holy " (Lev.
21:22). There is a difference between lameness and
leprosy and the Lord means us to regard it. A believer
may be dark on many things and yet not defiled. One
may fail to " keep rank " and yet not be unfit to hold
communion with God. Such have a place in the Church
of God and at the table. As one weak in the faith the saints
are commanded to " receive " him (Rom. 14:1), then to
" support " him (1 Thess. 5:14). The Churches of God
ought to be to the " weak " and the " feeble " as the
" inn " was to the wounded man who was found on the
road to Jericho. There are many of the dear saints of
God who are lame, not so much from their own fault as
from the fault of those who had the care of them, during
their spiritual infancy. We read of one Mephibosheth
who was lame for life because a careless nurse let him

fall when a babe. Yet he sat at the King's table as one of his sons. May the Lord preserve the balance of His truth within our souls, and help us to discriminate between weakness and defilement.

Every Sabbath was the time appointed for the priesthood to assemble at the table. On the first day of every week the disciples of the Lord habitually met to break bread and drink the wine (Acts 20:7). There was "the Lord's day" and "the Lord's Supper" (Rev. 1:10; 1 Cor. 11:20); or, as it may be read, "the Lordly day" and "the Lordly Supper," the "day" for the "supper" and the "supper" for the "day" both being distinguished by a word occurring nowhere else in the New Testament. It is clear, moreover, from the record given, that the early churches gathered to break the bread and drink the wine on the first of every week. They had no "Ordinance day" or "Communion Sundays." Every resurrection day witnessed the gathered company at the feast, and so should it be with us to-day. The times have changed, and so have the customs of men, but the Word of the Lord is sure and steadfast for ever. Beloved! let us cleave to it firmly, seeking to act it out in the fear of the Lord.

Golden Candlestick

(Exodus 25:31-39)

The third and last vessel in the Holy Place was the Golden Candlestick, or lampstand. It was a vessel of pure gold, consisting of a shaft, an upright centre branch, and six other branches proceeding out of the shaft, three on either side. On the end of each of the seven branches was a lamp of gold containing pure olive oil, and these were to be kept continually burning to give light within the Holy Place. It was the only source of light there, and in that light the priesthood served and worshipped Jehovah.

It stood on the south side of the Holy Place, over against the table of shewbread.

There are deep and precious truths foreshadowed in this golden lampstand, upon which our souls may meditate

Golden Candlestick

with joy and blessing. Christ personally is and ever was " *the* Life " and " *the* Light." Life and light Divine have their source and manifestation in His blessed Person. He, and He only, is the Giver of life and light, and He has communicated both unto His saints. They are in possession of His life, and "children of the light," and it is through them that He manifests and displays Himself. The candlestick seems to point to that deep, mysterious oneness that exists between the Head and the members of the "one new Man," expressively called "the Christ" (see 1 Cor. 12:12, Greek).

There are no dimensions given for this vessel, but it was to be beaten out of a talent of gold. It was of *pure* gold ; there was no tinsel or alloy. This marks the Divine character of the truth contained in the type. It reminds us of the Church as formed and created in His image, the workmanship of God.

It was of *beaten* work. Beating is the emblem of sorrow and suffering. This points to the sufferings of the cross as the birthplace of the Church. It was during the process of beating that the various branches of this golden lampstand, with their flowers and bowls, were formed. They were all hid, as it were, in that unbeaten talent, but as the hammer was brought down upon it by a skilful hand, one after another of the branches was produced, until it stood complete before the maker's eye one solid work of beaten gold. It was thus the Church was formed. The "deep sleep" into which the Lord God put the first Adam, while He builded out of his side "the woman" who was to be his partner ; the corn of wheat falling into the ground to die and bear much fruit ; and this beating out of the golden lampstand all foreshadow the deep and bitter sufferings of the cross, to which the Church, as the body and the bride of Christ, owes her existence. The talent of gold was ever valuable and precious in itself, but, apart from the beating of it, there could have been no golden lampstand. And but for the bruising and death of the Son of God—the Second Adam—there could have been no Church—no second Eve—to become His Body and His Bride.

The lampstand consisted of three parts, viz., the shaft, the six branches, and the branch. The shaft was the base of all. Out of it came six side branches, and also the center and upright branch. The word translated " shaft " is rendered " thigh " in Gen. 24:2, and " loins " in Gen. 46:26. As the children came from the loins of Jacob, so came the branches from this *shaft*. It gave them being. They came forth from it, having, as it were, its life, its nature, and its beauty as their own. So comes the Church from Christ. She is possessed of His life and adorned in His beauty. " He that sanctifieth and they who are sanctified are all *of one*," even as the branches were of the same gold as the shaft out from which they came :—" For which cause He is not ashamed to call them brethren " (Heb. 2:11). Wondrous dignity ! He is the Firstborn from the dead : they are His brethren. He is the Son of God : they are the sons of God. His Father is their Father, His God their God. Christ is the Head of the Church : the Church is the fulness of Christ. She is called to be a co-heir and joint-inheritor with Him. She is the Eve of the Second Adam. She is quickened, and raised, and seated together with Him, a partaker of His life, possessed of His Spirit, and presently to share His Glory.

The six branches sprang *out from* the shaft, three on either side. They were not artificially fastened on to it, but they came out from it. Such is the union of Christ and His members. It is compared to a body of many members, all having the same life, and united by a common bond to the living Head. As Eve was taken from the side of Adam, possessed of his life, his very counterpart, so in wondrous grace hath the Church been formed *from* and *for* her Lord. The same life is in the feeblest member as is in the Head, and not one of these members can ever be severed from Him, or perish. I do not see how any one can believe the Bible, and hold what is commonly known as " falling-away doctrine." In such a gospel there is no vital union with Christ. The believer is looked upon as artificially united to Him, and liable to lose his hold and drop into hell at any time. This doctrine robs Christ of His glory, and the believer of his peace. Texts bearing on the believer's *warfare* (as 1 Cor. 9:27) or *fruitfulness* (as John 15:6) are pressed into service to prove that a believer may finally perish. But we know from such Scriptures as 1 Cor. 6:17 ; Eph. 5:30 ; Rom. 7:4, that the believer is *everlastingly* united to the risen Christ, and that he can *never* be separated from Him (see Rom. 8: 35-39 ; John 10:28). And these Scriptures cannot be broken, neither can they contradict themselves.

In each of the six branches, there were bowls made like unto almonds, with a knop and a flower of gold. The almond-like bowl or calyx reminds us of the resurrection. The almond tree is the first to show its bud in Spring. It is the first to wake up, as in resurrection, after the dreary winter. The rod of Aaron laid up before the Lord during the night, had *in the morning* the bud, the blossom, and the fruit of the almond upon it. How sweetly these emblems remind us of the resurrection of the Son of God and of the formation and resurrection of the Church with Him. Around the dark shadow of His cross, and the still darker portal of the tomb, the lonely women watched and wept. It seemed as if the winter had set in without a hope of Spring's return to them. But on the early dawn of the resurrection morning the opening bud was seen, and the Risen One appeared to their joy, linking them with Himself, and saying " Go to My *brethren*, and say unto them, I ascend to *My* Father and *your* Father, to *My* God and *your* God." The corn of wheat had died, to live in the fruitfulness of resurrection. The rod laid up in death before the Lord had borne its fruit, on that resurrection morning (John 20:17). Like the branches springing out of the almond-like calyx, and like the almonds found on the rod of Jehovah's chosen priest, the Church is the fruit of Christ's death and resurrection, and is raised and seated and blessed together with Him. Drawing their sap from Him, as the branches from the vine, they bear the fruit of righteousness, and " the life of Jesus " is manifest in " their mortal bodies " (2 Cor. 4:11).

The center stem is called " *his* branch " (see Exod. 37:17, where the word is given in the singular), distinguishing it from the six side branches. Its place in the midst, with its pre-eminence and beauty, reminds us of the fact that although Christ has linked His saints with Him and calls them " brethren," yet in all things He has the pre-eminence. He is the Head, the Chiefest among the ten thousand, Fairer than the children of men, Altogether lovely. He may call the objects of His grace by the endearing name of " brethren," but they call Him " Lord," and own His place in the midst, as Center and Source of all.

The lamps were filled with pure olive oil. Oil is the type of the Holy Spirit, and the lamp filled with this may indicate that fulness of the Spirit which believers now possess, and which it is their privilege and responsibility daily to enjoy (Eph. 5:18).

The many lamps gave only one *light* (Exod. 25:37), and its chief use was to shine over against the face of the candlestick, displaying its beauties. The saints filled with the Spirit do not exhibit themselves or speak of their own comeliness. They bear witness to the worth of Jesus. Stephen, *full* of the Holy Ghost, looked steadfastly up to Heaven and said, " I see Jesus." Peter, *filled* with the Spirit, testified of the dead and risen Christ ; and when the Church is all complete and glorified with Christ in

Heaven, she will still be the vessel in whom and by whom Christ will be revealed. A believer full of the Holy Ghost will have the eye turned up to Christ, and not down or into self. He will speak of Christ, and not of his own perfection or sanctity. When Moses came down from the mount, the glory of God was beaming in his face, and everybody saw it and knew it, yet *He* "wist" it not. Thus the golden lampstand stood before the Lord, shedding forth its light continually, and thus before God's face for ever shall stand in wondrous union, Divine beauty, and unfading light, the Church as the body and the bride of Christ.

But there is another aspect in which this golden lampstand may be viewed. It has a place to fill on earth, amid the darkness of the night. When John, the beloved disciple who had leaned upon Immanuel's bosom at the Supper, was in Patmos' lonely isle, he was called to behold seven golden candlesticks. They were not within the heavens, but scattered throughout Asia Minor, as witnesses for God, in a dark and guilty world. They were the bearers of Divine light down here among men, and the Lord Jesus, clad in priestly robes, was seen moving amongst them, constantly watching over them, caring for them, praising them and rebuking them as they had need. Like the beloved disciple himself, the Church has a double place to fill; up there in the bosom of the Lord, down here in a cold and evil world. The Church, as the body of Christ, is divinely perfect and divinely united : it can never be tarnished or divided. " The Churches of God " on earth are liable to fail, and they may receive either praise or blame from Him who walks among them. As Aaron trimmed the lamps, pouring in the oil and using the tongs and snuffers, so Christ, as He walked amidst these churches, had words of grace and cheer to some, and of warning and reproof to others. The trimming of the wick—the use of the tongs and snuffers—is quite as necessary as the fresh supply of oil, in order to have a clear and shining light, and the Lord knows in what proportions to give the ministry of grace, and the word of faithful rebuke. In some of the assemblies there was little to correct, in others little to approve. But so long as they were His, He trimmed and fed the lamps as they had need. May the Churches of God and the saints individually have the willing ear to hear His voice whether He speak rebuke or cheer. Thus shall they continue as His light-bearers on the earth. Each candlestick stood on its own base and had a separate existence of its own. There was no human confederation of churches or earthly seat of government. Each church was responsible to Christ alone. Yet He who is in the midst of each separate assembly and unites around Himself all who are in it, is here seen walking in the midst of the seven assemblies uniting them all. They were all watched over by the same All-seeing Eye, and trimmed by the same Almighty Hand. So long as the churches remained true to Him, or had an ear to hear His voice, He governed them Himself. But when they ceased to hear His voice and to repent of their sins, He disowned them, and removed their candlestick out of its place (Rev. 21:5). He alone can do this. It is not man's work.

This puts the Churches of God in a deeply solemn position as His witness and light-bearers down here on earth. If the spiritual condition of the individuals who compose these churches be right, with God, and if the saints are living in communion with Him, each subject to Christ as Lord and to His Word, there will be little fear, but the lampstand will give a clear and shining light. The truth of God will be upheld. Christ's Name will be honored. His gospel will be sounded forth, and sinners will be saved. His Word will be proclaimed and taught, and should evil raise it head, it will be dealt with in His fear. Happy the church and the individual saint, thus abiding in His love and watched over by His eye, fed and trimmed by His hand, and standing as a luminary amid earth's darkest night, waiting for the dawn of the resurrection morning.

THE HOLIEST OF ALL

The Veil

(Exodus 26:31-33)

The Veil divided between the Holiest of All—the immediate presence-chamber of Jehovah—and the Holy Place, the place of priestly worship and service.

It was a curtain of blue, purple, scarlet, and fine linen, with cherubims. It was upheld by four pillars of shittim wood, set on silver sockets, with suspending hooks of gold. So long as the veil remained unrent, the priest was shut out from the immediate presence of his God, and the Divine glory was hidden from his gaze. Only once a year, the high priest was permitted to enter, and that, alone, with the blood of atonement in his hand, and his person en-shrouded by a cloud of holy incense.

The Holy Ghost has interpreted this type for us in His own words, as found in Heb. 10:20. We read there, "The *veil,* that is to say, *His flesh.*" This veil, then, foreshadowed the "flesh," or the humanity of the Lord Jesus. " God as manifest in the *flesh* " (1 Tim. 3:16) ; " and the Word became *flesh* and tabernacled among us " (John 1:14). What a mystery of grace lies here before us, in the consideration of which we need to proceed with bowed heads and reverent spirits, reining in our imagin-ation, and being guided by the light of Holy Scripture. He was the Holy One as regards His humanity ; unlike all other men, inasmuch as He was sinless ; yet so near to us did He come, that we are told, " Forasmuch then as the children are partakers of flesh and blood, He also

The High Priest of Israel on the
Great Day of Atonement

Himself likewise took part of THE SAME " (Heb. 2:14).
His incarnation was a necessity in order that He might
die, and so was His perfectness in order that He might
die *for us* to redeem us. There was no gold entwined
amid the colours of the vail, as we see it in the texture of
the ephod of the priest, for that would indicate His
Divinity and humanity were intermingled. But such was
not the case. He, was thirsty at the well of Sychar, and
hungry in the wilderness, and He *felt* them both. He was
weary with His journey, and He rested Himself and slept
on a pillow in the boat. O how blessed to know that we
have such a Jesus ! So tender that both the babe and the
beloved disciple might lie close to His bosom and feel
that they were at home, and yet withal He was the Mighty
God—Emmanuel. The hooks of gold by which the vail
were suspended may speak of this, while the cherubim
wrought in the blue, the purple, and the scarlet, may
indicate the presence of the Divine power that was in Him,
oftentimes exerted on behalf of others, but never for Himself.

It was upheld and displayed by four pillars, cut off,
uncrowned, and set on silver sockets. There are four
Gospels giving a divinely-inspired revelation of Christ's
holy birth and life, all ending with His cutting off upon
the Cross. We need no other " Life of Christ " to supple-
ment them. Many have been written, bearing the infirmities of their authors' opinions, in contradiction of the
inspired words of the Holy Ghost.

But the veil in all its beauty afforded no access to the
presence of God, but rather barred the way. And the
incarnation of Christ, apart from His death, would not of
itself have brought the sinner nigh to God. We need to
remember this, because there are many who occupy the
place of teachers in the professing church, who are now
saying that we are united to Christ in His incarnation,

that God is the Father of all men, whether they have
been born again or not, and that as a consequence all
men will be saved. But there can be no union with Christ
save in the new creation; no entrance to the family of
God but by a new second birth; and no place in Heaven
but on the ground of redemption. The veil had to be rent,
ere the way was opened into the presence of God, and
Christ had to die ere sinners could be "made nigh" by
blood (Eph. 2:13). At the very moment of the death of
God's holy Lamb outside the gate of Jerusalem, the veil
within the Temple was rent "in the midst" from top
to bottom, and the graves of the saints were opened.
The former of these signs giving the pledge of access to
God, the other, of the destruction of death, and both of
these, fruits of the death of Christ. Blessed be God, there
is no barrier now! The inner and outer courts are both
open to the saints of God, and the whole range of spiritual
blessings in heavenly places, has been, through grace,
made theirs. The saints "draw nigh" to pray and praise,
and within the inner circle, in the fulness of light and
love Divine, they sing—

> "Within the Holiest of all,
> Cleansed by His precious blood,
> Before Thy throne Thy children fall,
> And worship Thee—our God."

The Ark

(Exodus 25:10-16)

The only vessel within the circle of the Holiest was
the Ark with its Mercy Seat. We find it described in
Exodus 25:10-21. It was a chest or coffer made of
shittim wood, overlaid within and without with pure gold.
It had a crown or band of gold around its top, a golden
ring on each of its four corners, and two staves of shittim

wood overlaid with gold wherewith it might be carried through the desert. Within this Ark lay the two tables of the law ; and, later on, we find there was a golden pot with manna, and the budded rod of Aaron deposited within it.

Here, as elsewhere, we see the God-man in the gold and the shittim wood. The unbroken tables within the Ark remind us of the perfect obedience of Christ. We are at once reminded of the words, true only of Him of whom the Ark is a type—" I delight to do Thy will, O My God ; yea, Thy law is within My heart " (Psa. 40:8). There, and only there, had God's will its dwelling-place. Of Him, and Him alone can it be said that He loved the Lord His God with *all* His heart, and soul, and strength, and mind, and that He did so continuously and constantly. The first two tables were broken beneath the mount by Moses when he saw the people engaged in worshipping the calf of gold. Of what use could such a law have been to them ! Its first commandment claimed complete allegiance to God ; its second forbade the making of a graven image ; and its third the taking of God's name in vain. While Moses was on the way from God to the people with these commands, what were they doing ? They had made a graven image, they were doing homage there before it, and declaring it to be the God who had redeemed them. Such was the reception given by man to God's most holy law, and such is man's treatment of it still. His rebellious heart is estranged from God—it is not subject to His law, nor can it be. The tables are broken, and, with fallen man, they can never be renewed. How foolish, then, for men to think that by observing fragments of a broken law they can satisfy God, or justify themselves. Yet how many seek by such a path to reach the Kingdom of God, and how zealously they cling to outward forms and mingle law and grace. How strangely

it must sound in Heaven to hear from congregations
Sunday after Sunday, chanted in a single breath, such
words as, " Incline our hearts to keep Thy *law*," followed
by, " Save us by Thy *grace*." But salvation is not a com-
plex thing made up of law and grace, else grace were no
more grace. The sinner has broken the law of God, and
thus forfeited every claim to righteousness on that ground.
Moreover, he is under its curse and awaiting its punishment. But there was One—different from all others—in
whose heart the claims of God had their honoured place.
And He was " Jesus Christ the Righteous." Perfect in
His unswerving fidelity to God and in His love to men.
In Him the claims of a holy God were fully met and all
His righteous requirements satisfied.

The Mercy Seat
(Exodus 25:17-22)

The lid of the Ark was made of pure gold, with cherubim of gold on its ends, and is called the Mercy-Seat.
The wings of the cherubim overshadowed the Ark, and
their faces looked to each other toward the Mercy-Seat.
The word for Mercy-Seat signifies " to atone," or " cover,"
and in the New Testament it is rendered " propitiation "
(see Rom. 3:25).   God's mercy can only be known in
Christ, and on the ground of atonement. If it is to be
extended to sinners, it must be in consistency with God's
holiness, and if grace is to take its place upon the throne,
it must reign in righteousness. But how is this to be ?
The only way possible is on the ground of atonement.
And to this the Cross of Christ is the all-sufficient answer.
There, all apparently irreconcilable attributes of God are
harmonised and blended, in their Divine perfection and
beauty. There, " mercy and truth are met together,
righteousness and peace have kissed each other " (see

Psalm 85:10). There "mercy rejoices against judgment."

On the great day of atonement—Israel's annual cleansing from sin—Aaron the priest, robed in linen garments, entered within the veil, with the blood of a sin-offering. This was sprinkled on the Mercy-Seat once, and before it seven times. *Once* was enough for the eye of Jehovah, but seven times—the perfect number—for the eye of the worshipper. *We* need to be reminded often of the perfectness of the atonement of Christ, but in the estimate of God it is ever the same. The importance of this act cannot be over-estimated. It was not a question of some single act of transgression : that would have been settled at the altar in the Court. But the question uppermost in the Day of Atonement was—" How can a holy God continue to dwell in the midst of a sinful and failing people ? How can His throne be established in righteousness in their midst ? " The answer was found in the sprinkled blood. It was there, on the blood-stained Mercy-Seat, that the Shekinah rested and it was concerning this same spot that Jehovah said, " There will I *meet* with thee, and *commune* with thee."

How blessed it is for our souls to grasp the antitype of all this, as we have it in the death of Christ. True, we often sing—

> " His precious blood is sprinkled there,
> *Before* and *on* the throne."

but how far have we individually really learned of the perfect satisfaction of God, and of the deep, eternal rest that He Himself has found in the death of His own beloved Son ? Beloved young saints, this is where you need to begin, if you would enjoy deep and settled peace and know anything of real communion with God. If you do not see a satisfied, yea, a well-pleased and resting God, the probability is that the accuser will roar against you,

telling you of your past offences and your present unworthiness, and drive you from the solace of the secret
place, where the wings of the Almighty stretch themselves
out to protect you from Satan's power. But, gazing on
that precious blood, we see the perfect answer to all we
have done, and to all that we are. We learn there that the
blood of the slain Lamb has given entire satisfaction to
God, and covered all our guilt, leaving nothing but its
own preciousness on the spot. How boldly, then do our
souls face the tempter's rage, and how intelligently do we
sing—

> " I hear the accuser roar
>   Of ills that I have done :
> I know them well, and thousands more—
>   *Jehovah findeth none.*"

And not only does the blood *bring* us there, but, blessed
be God, it *keeps* us there. If our souls are dwelling in the
light of God, and accustoming themselves to say, " Search
me, O God," we will find that there is much within us
still, that is contrary to the circle of infinite holiness in
which we stand. Then, how are we to abide in its searching
light ? Just because the blood is there. The blood *cleanseth*
us from all sin. That does not mean that it takes sin out
of us. To think so, God says, would be self-deception.
But while we are walking there in God's holy presence,
the blood speaks *for us*, and, in spite of all that we feel
ourselves to be, we are *counted clean* for its sake. And
at the blood-stained Mercy-Seat we commune with God.
Covet the enjoyment of this, ye beloved young Christians.
It is more to be desired than much fine gold. It will give
you strength for the journey home, and there, communing
at God's Mercy-Seat and throne of grace, you will renew
your strength and mount up as on eagle's wings.

The cherubim looked down upon the blood-stained
Mercy-Seat, acquiescing and admiring. Some think they

represent angels, others, saints. No doubt the host above do greatly admire the great redemption work of Christ, but, being all of gold and of the same piece as the Mercy-Seat, we rather think they are symbols of the Divine majesty and power of God. At Eden's gate they stand connected with the sword of justice to bar the way. But here, at the Mercy-Seat, they welcome the sinner's approach. There is no sword now. It has been sheathed in the Victim, and they gaze upon the blood. Blessed exchange ! We fear them now no more, but rather cry, " I will abide in Thy tabernacle for ever : I will trust in the covert of Thy *wings* " (Psa. 61:4). " Because Thou hast been my refuge, therefore in the *shadow of Thy wings* will I rejoice " (Psa. 63:7).

The *rings* and *staves* speak of the pilgrim character. If God's saints are wanderers in the desert, He will be with them all the way. The Ark accompanied them throughout. It stood in Jordan's dried-up bed, until they crossed in safety. It compassed the walls of Jericho. Then, when the wilderness was past and the conflicts over, it was carried into the Temple and deposited on the golden floor, and its staves were then *drawn out*. The pilgrim host had reached their home. And so shall we, beloved. Till then, we have God with us and for us.

The FLOOR of the Tabernacle was *sand*. Above and around the glories of Christ have filled the eye; but below, there was nothing but the desert sand. The priest stood within the holy circle, surrounded by the shadows of heavenly things, but, like ourselves, he was literally in the desert. We are reminded daily that this is not our rest. But the Holy City with the golden street is yonder, gleaming in the distance, with its glory and its song. To this let our pilgrim steps press on. Burning sands and deserts with thorns, may hurt our wearied feet, but an hour with our Lord, will make up for it all. The rest and calm of that bright home awaits us, and a warm welcome by the Lord of the place. " For the Lord Himself shall descend from Heaven with a shout, with the voice of the archangel and with the trump of God, and the dead in Christ shall rise first. Then WE, who are alive and *remain* unto the coming of the Lord, shall be caught up together with them in the clouds to meet the Lord in the air. *So* shall we ever be *with* the Lord." (1 Thess. 4:16-17).

The Ark and Mercy Seat

THE SERVANTS

Levites and Their Work

The Levites are typical of believers as " the *servants* of Jesus Christ." Their work was to bear the Tabernacle and the holy vessels through the desert, to set it up according to the Divine pattern in the divinely ordered place, and to take it down when the cloud arose for the journeying of the camp. Their call, their qualification for service, and the various spheres to which Jehovah appointed them, are all subjects of interest, upon which we may meditate with profit to our souls.

The *natural* character—as we may call it—of Levi is well described in the words of his father, Jacob, as recorded in Genesis 49:5-7. Cruel, self-willed and fierce, cursed and scattered, yet by God's grace picked out to become the chosen servant of the house of God—according to nature, unfit for the presence of God or the fellowship of His people. " O my soul, come not thou into their secret ; unto their assembly, mine honour, be not thou *united*," yet by grace the union with Simeon is dissolved, and Levi is " joined " to God's high priest   (Num. 18: 2-4), to minister unto him and " to do the service of the tabernacle." Their standing according to nature is set aside : they are called according to grace to fill the place of · Israel's firstborn (Num. 3:12, 13),   a typically dead and risen people, alive unto God, in new circumstances, with new surroundings. Thus it is that the call of God and the grace of God hath come to us sinners of the Gentiles who were " afar off," having no hope " and without God in the world," quickening us together with Christ that we might be joined to the Lord and become one spirit with Him. Able, like one of old to say—" By the grace of God, I am what I am "—" Whose I am, and whom I serve " (1 Cor. 15:10 ; Acts 27:23).

Next to their call, comes their preparation for service. Being brought nigh unto God, they must be in a condition suited to that new position, and, having received a ministry in the Lord, they must be qualified and furnished so that they may fulfil it. As we meditate on what the Levites required to fit them for their ministry, we shall learn what is still required of those who would acceptably serve the Lord in His Gospel and His House.

They were to be *"cleansed"* and *"separated"* in the presence of the whole assembly. This was the first step. Not " education " and " ordination," but " cleansing " and " separation." This accords with that " washing of regeneration " and conversion to God, so frequently enjoined upon all who would serve the Lord Christ. Apart from these, no sinner ever can become a servant of God. Men who have never been born again may be voted into places of ecclesiastical power by the fellows, or appointed to them by their patrons ; they may preach and teach and " administer the sacraments," but without God's call and His qualifications for service, they are the servants of Satan. Nor is conversion the *only* qualification that God requires. The Levites, having been cleansed by another, were afterwards to shave their flesh and wash their clothes and so " make themselves clean." This accords with the words written to those who had already been separated from the unequal yokes and fellowships of darkness   (see 2 Cor. 6:14-17),   being received of God for His service here. " Having therefore these promises, beloved, let us cleanse ourselves from all defilement of flesh and spirit, perfecting holiness in the fear of God " (2 Corinthians 7:1).   There is much to " lay aside " (1 Peter 2:1) and to " put off " (Col. 3:8, 9) after being converted, and thus the believing one is " proved " and " blameless " before he publicly serves (1 Tim. 3:10). They were given then to Aaron as a gift (Num. 8:19, with John 17:6), and by him back to Jehovah as an offering (Num. 8:21, with John 17:10, 11). Then, they were allowed to enter upon the service of the Tabernacle for a brief period of five-and-twenty years (Num. 8:24).

They had no earthly inheritance given them as their brethren of the tribes of Israel. Jehovah Himself was their inheritance, and of His offerings they were allowed to partake (Deut. 18:1, 2). Their wants were bountifully supplied by their God through their brethren, and they lacked no good thing (Num. 35:4-8). It was thus with the servants of Christ in early days. An Apostle then was not ashamed to confess, " Silver and gold have I none " (Acts 3:6), while another tells of the " loss of all things" for Christ's honored name, and produces as the credentials of his Apostleship the hunger, the thirst, the nakedness, and the stripes that he endured in his path of service for God's Gospel and His truth. Men of those days served not for worldly advantage of " filthy lucre." " The ministry " was no fashionable trade in which the praise of men with worldly titles and emoluments were secured. " Bonds and afflictions " (Acts 20:23) were God's servants' portion and prospects : a " dying daily " (1 Cor. 15:31) the only " living." It remained for a day of apostasy from the truth for professed " ministers of God " to wander forth, to and fro, seeking a " place," like that Levite of Bethlehem-Judah who came to Micah's house and bargained with him to become his priest, for which he received a yearly salary, a suit of apparel, and his victuals. For this remuneration he was " content " to stay and officiate as the family priest, until the larger sphere of becoming priest to a tribe presented itself. The modern custom answering to this ancient story is too well-known to require to be pointed out. The only wonder is, that true saints of God should be found perpetuating and supporting such a God-dishonouring system, at which sceptics point with contempt and scorn, in evidence of the sham of modern Christianity. But the pattern and example of true ministry abides in the written Word, and by these we are called upon to test who ever assumes the prerogative of being " a minister of Jesus Christ " among His people.

Division of Labor

The tribe of Levi was divided into three families : Kohath, Gershon and Merari. To each of these a part of God's Tabernacle was entrusted. There was diversity and division of labor, combined with unity of purpose and action. Every man had his place given him by Jehovah. He knew it, and kept it. Every man had his own peculiar work for which he was fitted, and all went on under the supervision of God's high priest (Num. 4:27-33) without a jar or murmur. The family of Merari had the boards, the bars, the pillars and the sockets, as their burden. When the cloud rested for the encampment of the tribes, they were the first workmen on the spot where Jehovah's dwelling-place was to be reared. Their first work would be to lay down the heavy silver sockets on the bare sand of the desert. These formed the foundation of God's house. The shittim boards were next raised and fitted into the sockets, each in its appointed place, and finally the bars that framed the several boards together were passed through the golden rings. When the work of the family of Merari was ended, their brethren of the family of Gershon began their work. To them was committed the curtains, the coverings, the hangings, and the cords—that which beautified and sheltered the work of the sons of Merari. The service of these two families was very closely related : they were true "yoke-fellows" and "laborers together of God" (1 Cor. 3:9).

They walked together on the journey (Num. 10:17), and labored together in the work of building God's house. Later still, the sons of Kohath came, bearing on their shoulders the holy vessels—the ark, the table, the candlestick and the altars in their coverings of purple, blue, scarlet and badgers' skins (Num. 3:29-32 ; 4:2). They found a tabernacle already built and beautified. Their ministry was for the furnishing of the house and its courts, for worship and for sacrifice.

All this has its significance to us of later times, and we may meditate upon it with profit and blessing. May the Lord enable us to do so in His fear. Here we have God's principles of ministry in connection with the building of His ancient house, and these principles are not departed from but rather accentuated and emphasised in New Testament Scriptures, and in the present work of the Lord, in the building of His dwelling-place of present time, even that house which is " the church of the living God " (1 Tim. 3:15)   and " habitation of God in the Spirit " (Eph. 2:22).

Ministry: Evangelists, Pastors, Teachers

The appointments of God regarding ministry are here seen in type in the services of the three families of the sons of Levi.

The Merarites, with their foundations and framework, represent the *evangelist* and his work ; the Gershonites, with their curtains, coverings and cords, strengthening, shielding and beautifying, the *pastor* and his work ; the Kohathites, bearing with steady step the various vessels of the sanctuary, and placing them in due order, the *teacher* and his ministry.

The sphere of the evangelist is the wide world : sinners wherever he can find them are his congregation : the Gospel of the grace of God is his message. Like the Merarite of old, he bears the silver sockets of redemption, as the only foundation for the sinner. He goes forth guided by the Spirit of God into the world and speaks of Christ crucified. This is his theme, He lays the sockets on the desert sands. World-reformation is not his mission ; precedent and " stepping-stone " to the Gospel of God he knows nothing of. He preaches Christ : Christ as the Savior, Christ as the Lord, Christ as the foundation of salvation for the sinner (Acts 4:12), Christ as the foundation of the Church (Matt. 16:18) and of the fellowship of the saints (1 Cor. 3:11). Then, having presented Christ, he seeks to bring sinners to Him, that they may accept Him as Savior and own Him as Lord. His aim is to "make disciples" (Matt. 28:19). And, having by the power of the Gospel, accomplished this, he next gathers the saved ones together as the Lord has commanded (Matt. 18:20), and builds them according to the Divine pattern, given in the Book. It was thus that " the churches " of early times were formed. There was the preaching of " Christ Crucified " (1 Cor. 2:2), the laying of the foundation of the assembly (1 Cor. 3:10), and the " preaching of the Word " (Acts 18:11) to those whom God had saved and gathered together. All this was embraced in the " work of an evangelist " in days of old. In modern evangelism he is said to " preach the Gospel only," whatever this may mean. If God gives blessing in the conversion of sinners, he is not expected to have anything further to say to them, certainly not to gather or build them together as God had appointed, but rather to move on, as the ostrich who leaveth her eggs in the sand, where the foot of man may crush them (Job 39:14, 15).

The Merarites' work was immediately followed by that of their fellow-labourers the Gershonites, who with the cords strengthened, with the coverings sheltered, and with the curtains beautified what their brethren had builded. This is the work of the pastor. He co-operates with and follows up the evangelist. His work is to care for and shepherd the flock. To seek out the young, heal the broken and feed the standing still (Zech. 11:16). It was thus that Barnabas, " the Son of consolation "—a true Gershonite—followed up the " men of Cyrene " in their work at Antioch, exhorting the converts to " cleave " to the Lord (Acts 11:23). It was when this most blessed work had been neglected that the Lord lamented—" My tabernacle is spoiled, and all My *cords* are broken : My children are gone forth from Me and they are not : there is none to stretch forth My *tent* any more, and to set up My *curtains* for THE PASTORS are become brutish, and have not sought the Lord " (Jer. 10:20, 21). Words too sadly true, of our own time.

The Tabernacle being now set up and beautified, it remained for the sons of Kohath to carry in the holy vessels and put them in their ordered places in the house and courts of Jehovah. This is the work of the *teacher*. He brings in with wise and steady step, in their due order, and as the saints are able to hear, the truths of which these holy vessels are the types. The Brazen Altar telling of the Perfect Sacrifice and the believer's acceptance in Christ ; the Laver telling of his daily cleansing, and on to the antitypes of the Altar, the Table and the Candlestick—the standing of the saints as risen with Christ, worshipping at the Altar, feeding at the Table, communing at the

Mercy-Seat. And thus by steady, continuous "toil *in* the Lord" does the "work *of* the Lord" go on from day to day and from age to age, in spite of man's opposition and Satan's hindrance. And thus it will continue until the time of wilderness warfare and service shall have run its course. Then as of old, when in the days of Solomon's glory the Levites exchanged the burdens of the Tabernacle and its vessels for rest and praise   (see 1 Chron. 23: 25-30) amid the glories of the Kingdom, so shall those who have served the Lord Jesus in His Gospel, His Church, and His Truth, receive in the millennial and eternal Kingdom and glory of their Lord, the reward of their labors and tears of the wilderness days. And there, amid the chaste glory of the eternal rest, where no tear of sorrow shall ever drop, or groan of pain be heard, where God is all in all, and the Lamb is all the glory—there " His *servants* shall serve Him, and they shall see His Face " (Rev. 22:3, 4).   Praise ye the Lord.

Amen and Amen

CPSIA information can be obtained at www.ICGtesting.com
Printed in the USA
BVOW012214040713

325141BV00007B/41/P

9 780825 436161